STUDIES IN ECONOMIC

This series, specially commissioned by the Economic History Society, provides a guide to the current interpretations of the main themes of economic and social history in which advances have recently been made or in which there has been significant debate.

Originally entitled 'Studies in Economic History', in 1974 the series had its scope extended to include topics in social history, and the new series title, 'Studies in Economic and Social History', signalises this development.

The series gives readers access to the best work done, helps them to draw their own conclusions in major fields of study, and by means of the critical bibliography in each book guides them in the selection of further reading. The aim is to provide a springboard to further work rather than a set of pre-packaged conclusions or short-cuts.

ECONOMIC HISTORY SOCIETY

The Economic History Society, which numbers over 3000 members, publishes the *Economic History Review* four times a year (free to members) and holds an annual conference. Enquiries about membership should be addressed to the Assistant Secretary, Economic History Society, Peterhouse, Cambridge. Full-time students may join at special rates.

STUDIES IN ECONOMIC AND SOCIAL HISTORY

Edited for the Economic History Society by L. A. Clarkson

PUBLISHED

OTHER TITLES ARE IN PREPARATION

Population Change in North-Western Europe, 1750–1850

Prepared for
The Economic History Society by

MICHAEL ANDERSON

Professor of Economic History,
University of Edinburgh

MACMILLAN
EDUCATION

First published 1988

Published by
MACMILLAN EDUCATION LTD
Houndmills, Basingstoke, Hampshire RG21 2XS
and London
Companies and representatives
throughout the world

Printed in Hong Kong

British Library Cataloguing in Publication Data
Anderson, Michael, *1942*–
Population change in North-western Europe,
1750–1850.—(Studies in economic and
social history).
1. Europe—Population—History
I. Title   II. Economic History Society
III. Series
304.6'094   HB3581
ISBN   0–333–34386–7

Series Standing Order

If you would like to receive future titles in this series as they are published, you can make use of our standing order facility. To place a standing order please contact your bookseller or, in case of difficulty, write to us at the address below with your name and address and the name of the series. Please state with which title you wish to begin your standing order. (If you live outside the United Kingdom we may not have the rights for your area, in which case we will forward your order to the publisher concerned.)

Customer Services Department, Macmillan Distribution Ltd
Houndmills, Basingstoke, Hampshire, RG21 2XS, England.

Contents

Acknowledgements

I could never have written this book without the help of many friends, students and colleagues, far too numerous to mention by name. I owe, however, special debts to Tony Wrigley and Roger Schofield, who have so patiently answered my many questions about their work over the years, to Ann-Sofie Kälvemark who at a critical point in my career made me aware of the rich opportunities that were present in the Swedish writings on historical demography, and to Rosalind Mitchison with whom I have so greatly enjoyed teaching a course on Western European demography and from whom I have learnt so much. Leslie Clarkson, Rab Houston and Elspeth Moodie made many helpful comments on earlier drafts of this book; for this I am very grateful even though I have at times been too stubborn to follow their wise advice. One invaluable source of counsel, Michael Flinn, in whose footsteps I have followed in so many ways, had sadly and prematurely died before the writing got under way. Through the generosity and kindness of his family, who gave most of his books and offprints to his old department in Edinburgh, I have nevertheless been able to benefit from the mass of material he collected and even, at times, from his trenchant marginalia. I should like to place on record here my appreciation of the generous gift of this material; it has made my task infinitely easier and more pleasurable.

Note on References

Numbered references in the text within square brackets relate to the entries in the Select Bibliography.

Editor's Preface

When this series was established in 1968 the first editor, the late Professor M. W. Flinn, laid down three guiding principles. The books should be concerned with important fields of economic history; they should be surveys of the current state of scholarship rather than a vehicle for the specialist views of the authors, and above all, they were to be introductions to their subject and not 'a set of pre-packaged conclusions'. These aims were admirably fulfilled by Professor Flinn and by his successor, Professor T. C. Smout, who took over the series in 1977. As it passes to its third editor and approaches its third decade, the principles remain the same.

Nevertheless, times change, even though principles do not. The series was launched when the study of economic history was burgeoning and new findings and fresh interpretations were threatening to overwhelm students – and sometimes their teachers. The series has expanded its scope, particularly in the area of social history – although the distinction between 'economic' and 'social' is sometimes hard to recognize and even more difficult to sustain. It has also extended geographically; its roots remain firmly British, but an increasing number of titles is concerned with the economic and social history of the wider world. However, some of the early titles can no longer claim to be introductions to the current state of scholarship; and the discipline as a whole lacks the heady growth of the 1960s and early 1970s. To overcome the first problem a number of new editions, or entirely new works, have been commissioned – some have already appeared. To deal with the second, the aim remains to publish up-to-date introductions to important areas of debate. If the series can demonstrate to students and their teachers the importance of the discipline of economic and social history and excite its further study, it will continue the task so ably begun by its first two editors.

The Queen's University of Belfast   L. A. CLARKSON
                                                        General Editor

List of Figures

1 The Problem

Between 1750 and 1850 the population of north-western Europe almost doubled. Rises on this scale had happened in the twelfth and thirteenth centuries, and also in the later fifteenth and sixteenth, but these periods had been punctuated by major crises, and had ended with setbacks in the hunger and plagues of the fourteenth and seventeenth centuries. As late as the 1690s Scotland and the Nordic countries experienced famines which reduced the population of parts of Scotland by at least 15 per cent and of some areas of Finland by over a quarter. The first half of the eighteenth century saw continuing problems. The Great Northern War of 1699–1721 brought dislocation and starvation to much of Scandinavia; perhaps a fifth of adult male Finns died. Smallpox killed a third of the population of Iceland in 1707. Many areas of France experienced famine in 1708–10. Plague rampaged through Denmark, Sweden, Finland and parts of Germany in 1708–12. England's population fell briefly in the 1720s and most of Europe experienced crisis in the early 1740s [2b; 3; 7; 16; 18].

By contrast, after 1750, there was a change, and after 1815 a very marked one (though the old world had not totally disappeared: Ireland experienced a disaster when the potato crop failed in the 1840s, and Finland a devastating crisis as late as 1867–8). In general, however, the period 1750–1850 was free from major demographic catastrophes, and even the lesser setbacks had little long-term effect. More strikingly, perhaps, this century of expansion was followed by more than a century of further growth. In many ways, between 1750 and 1850 Europe broke free from the demographic constraints of an earlier age [cf. 3; but see 43; 59].

How and why did this growth of population come about? What was its real significance? Our understanding of these problems has been transformed by work of the last twenty years. In this short book some of the issues and controversies that have emerged are outlined. Inevitably, in covering half a continent, some of the subtlety of local variation has been lost, and this is regrettable since an important lesson of recent research has been the demonstration of regional and international variations. Nevertheless, there are many similarities between the countries of our area; in particular, their late marriage patterns differed markedly from the Mediterranean and Eastern regions of the European continent [2a]. The significance of this special pattern of marriage behaviour provides a coherence and ultimately a conclusion for our theme.

2   Sources and Methods

Historical demography must, as a minimum, start from two kinds of information: numbers of people alive at different times, and the numbers of demographic events (births, deaths and migrations) experienced over time. Ideally, of course, more is required. To *understand* population development we need more data on the *mechanics* of changes than we can get from simple counts (and, in particular, information on the age patterns of deaths and migrations, the distributions of ages at which women bore children, changes in marriage ages and proportions ever marrying, and causes of death and how they were distributed across the population). To *explain* the changes we need to relate demographic information to its climatic, biological, economic and social contexts.

Unfortunately, for much of our period, really detailed basic information is often lacking; sometimes there is hardly any information at all. (The best general survey is [27]; see also [3; 6; 11; 15; 23].) In particular, over most of our area, regular, reliable, centrally organised population counts began only in the early nineteenth century. The main exceptions are the Nordic countries, though even here the accuracy of the earliest censuses has been questioned (Sweden's first census probably missed at least 60,000 people).

Elsewhere, regular censuses date from the early nineteenth century (for example every ten years from 1801 in England and Wales and in Scotland, but in Ireland effectively only from 1821). The French government made useful population counts in the 1690s, but then there is nothing of much use until the unstandardised collections of 1801 and 1806, followed, with more refined methods, by regular quinquennial counts from 1816. The conquests of the Napoleonic period led to the first nationally organised counts in Belgium and the Netherlands, in the Helvetic Republic (comprising most of modern Switzerland) and in some of the Germanic States. Thereafter, regular censuses began in Belgium in 1829, in the Netherlands in 1839, and in Switzerland in 1850. The first pan-Germanic census was in 1852.

Many of these early censuses are unsatisfactory since they failed to use two key aids to reliable counting: the collection of complete lists of the population including names and addresses; and the conducting of the whole census on one day. As a result, sometimes only very impressionistic estimates were made and, since the central authorities often did not even know how many communities existed, they had no check on the completeness of the data provided. Equally serious, the failure to complete the count of a country on a single day led to omission and double counting (the 1771 Dachsberg census of Bavaria was spread over ten years; the first British census of 1801 was spread over seven weeks). In addition, evasion was encouraged by widespread suspicion, sometimes justified, that censuses were to be used for taxation or military conscription purposes, though encouragement of over-counting was sometimes induced by beliefs (supposedly widespread in Ireland in 1831) that enumerators were to be paid according to the number of people they recorded [14b]. Even in the mid-nineteenth century many infants were under-reported and ages inaccurately stated.

Nevertheless, these early national censuses represent magnificent feats of organisation, equalled by few of the privately organised surveys which preceded them (the only clear exception is the count of the population of Scotland conducted in 1755 by Alexander Webster [11]). Most other pre-census population estimates come from counts of houses made for local taxation purposes, counts of adult males eligible for military conscription, or counts by church authorities of numbers of communicants. All these have unknown levels of omission, evasion and exemption; they also require us to guess appropriate 'multipliers' to inflate counts of houses or of adult males or of communicants to total population figures. As we shall see below, this inevitably leads to debate.

Regular efficient population counts had long been preceded by attempts to record quasi-demographic events. The church in many areas began the systematic recording of all baptisms in the late medieval period, and this gradually spread to marriages and burials as well (see e.g. [27; 6; 11; 23; 30]). Initially, however, these registers usually recorded not the demographic events of births and deaths but ecclesiastical events such as baptism, or burial in consecrated ground, or payments to church authorities; this led to major omissions – for example, of children who died before they could be baptised. Even 'marriage' registers are sometimes registers of *intention to* marry; they thus include reference to marriages which did not take place and record intent in the parish both of the bride and of the groom, thus leading to double counting.

By 1750, however, over most of Western Europe some parish records were kept; in some cases (e.g. France from 1579, the Nordic countries except Iceland from the 1730s) counts from the registers were regularly returned to central or local authorities. However, comprehensive central collection of information for demographic purposes (on births and deaths rather than burials and baptisms) generally came much later. Vital registration was secularised in France in 1792 but was for a long time very disorganised. Except during the Commonwealth, England and Wales had no State system until 1837 and even then births were under-registered. Scotland had to wait until 1855, Ireland until 1864. Even the excellent Swedish system needed modification in 1858.

The detail in which information was recorded varied widely [7; 11; 29; 30]. In mid-eighteenth-century England, for example, burial registers for adults frequently contain only a name and date, though the names of husbands of married women, and of at least one parent of children, are usually given. For baptisms and marriages more detail is often provided, but English information is minimal compared with that available in France or Sweden. In France, for example, a marriage register typically contained information on the names, ages, occupations and parents of the couple and also names of witnesses. French baptism registers nearly always gave enough detail to make the identification of parents unambiguous. Swedish registers by the 1820s were comprehensive and were supplemented by a continuously updated household register and by registers of in- and out-migration.

However, many registers are lost or incomplete. In Sweden, most places have surviving records of good quality and coverage. The other Nordic countries also have reasonable records, though in both Denmark and Finland up to 10 per cent of births were sometimes missed, and death recording was sometimes erratic, particularly for infants [31; 32]. In France, too, record quality, coverage and survival was high; infant and child deaths, however, were under-recorded especially in the mid-eighteenth century, and there were similar problems after the Revolution.

Elsewhere the position is less satisfactory. In Scotland, even where they had once been kept, most old parish registers have been lost or destroyed and the survivors are often of poor quality [11]. Welsh records raise many problems, but in England, Germany, Belgium and Switzerland there are many surviving registers which seem conscientiously kept, though the communities covered are unevenly spread across the country, and urban areas are poorly represented.

English registers, though, have other problems, relating especially to births and deaths (for a useful summary see [7, chaps 1–5]). Firstly (and between 1780 and 1820 in particular) baptisms by nonconformist ministers increased rapidly, and there was a steady expansion in the use of nonconformist burial grounds; relatively few of these nonconformist records survive, and indirect methods of estimation must be used. One recent estimate suggests that about 9 per cent of all children in the 1780s and about 16 per cent in the 1820s were baptised by nonconformist ministers; for burials the shortfalls are about 5 per cent and about 14 per cent respectively [7].

Secondly, over the eighteenth century in England the gap in time between birth and baptism steadily increased; by the 1790s the median gap was probably at least a month. This delay is important because high infant mortality meant that many children died before they could be baptised; since the burial of unbaptised children often went unrecorded, burial registration is also deficient. In the years 1750–1800 this factor alone may have reduced baptisms by 7 per cent below their 'proper' level and burials by 5 per cent; for 1800–37 the deficits were even higher.

Finally, rapid urban growth, and absenteeism among clergy led to widespread omissions from the English registers, especially of baptisms. Wrigley and Schofield estimate that about 5 per cent of births in the 1750s were not recorded by any church and by the early nineteenth century around one fifth [7]. In all, Wrigley and Schofield suggest that nonconformity, delayed baptism, and non-registration for other reasons, led to the Anglican registers by the early nineteenth century recording less than three-quarters of all births and deaths – though these estimates have been subjected to some criticisms [see e.g. 55]; comparable shortfalls for the 1750s are about 87 per cent of births and 93 per cent of deaths.

In spite of these problems, dramatic progress has been made in the exploitation of parochial records. We can distinguish two broad strategies, one based on 'family reconstitution', the other on forms of 'aggregative analysis' (a useful introduction is in [29]).

'Family reconstitution' begins by abstracting all baptisms, burials and marriages from a lengthy parish register run. The entries are sorted by name. Then, taking each marriage record in turn, an attempt is made to add to it information on the births and deaths of the couple, and on the births, deaths and marriages of their children. Where a complete record can be assembled it is possible to calculate a wide range of information including the ages of the couple at marriage, their ages at the birth of each of their children, and the birth intervals between children, and between marriage and the first child. Once these data are assembled for all possible couples in the community under study, a wide range of statistics relating to fertility, mortality (and especially infant and child mortality), age at marriage, and to some extent migration, can be derived.

Family reconstitution demands high-quality records. Omissions in birth recording distort estimates of fertility. Migration means that information on age at death or year of birth (and thus age at marriage) cannot be obtained (though Swedish records allow migrants to be traced to the registers of other parishes) [30]; also, if only records on non-migrants are used, there are questions about the representativeness of the group analysed. In addition, where only a small number of names was used in a community, it is impossible to relate each entry in a register to a single person or family, and as a result many 'ambiguous' entries arise. This is not a major problem in the detailed French and Scandinavian registers, but it causes difficulties in England and the Netherlands, and is a major barrier to work on Wales.

These problems mean that, even in France, the proportion of families on which information can be collected is often quite low, though the size of the 'reconstitutable minority' varies according to the topic under study. In thirteen English reconstitutions about 80 per cent of legitimate live births could be used for the calculation of infant mortality, but age-specific fertility rates could be calculated for only 16 per cent of all married women [9]. This accentuates another difficulty of community-based studies: because demographic events are inherently variable between families and over short periods of time, small numbers of observations mean that computed differences between places and periods may result from random fluctuations rather than reflecting 'real' differences in behaviour [28].

It is not, however, easy to expand the number or scale of family reconstitutions since the work is time-consuming and computerisation has proved, until recently, difficult. In Germany, Sweden and Belgium the work of earlier generations of genealogists has been utilised to speed the task [33; 34; 81]. In Germany, for example, over 100 'Ortssippenbücher' exist; these 'Collections of family histories of the residents of a particular place' provide genealogies on all residents in a village in as far as these can be compiled from village records [82; 83].

Nevertheless, several hundred communities in Western Europe have now been reconstituted for our period (see [3] for examples to 1979), though the scatter of parishes covered is uneven, with communities often selected because of good records or personal interest rather than as part of an overall plan; the main exceptions here are a major French project for the systematic analysis of a representative sample of forty communities spread across the entire country, and Swedish work on a large, statistically stratified sample of parishes from the south of the country [22; 43]. In England, by mid-1986, nearly thirty parishes had been reconstituted by the Cambridge Group alone, although some of these reconstitutions have not been wholly successful and most do not go past 1837 (when parish registration falls off markedly in completeness) while some stop at 1811.

Family reconstitution is invaluable but it has limitations. In particular, unless population mobility is low it cannot produce statistics which require knowledge of 'numbers at risk'. It thus provides good information on infant mortality but not on the death rates of adults, allows estimation of average ages at marriage but not of proportions ultimately marrying, and is little help in determining the population of a community, let alone national populations.

As a result, alongside family reconstitution, work has continued on 'aggregative analysis'. The basis of aggregative analysis is simple: take a high-quality register of reasonable continuity; count, for each year, the numbers of baptisms, burials and marriages. The resulting figures (and particularly the differences between numbers of baptisms and burials) provide important clues about long-run population change; study of short-run fluctuations in burials shows patterns of mortality crises; examination of the seasonality of the burials, and study of correlations of changes in baptisms and marriages with changes in burials, provide clues about the causes of the crises.

Beginning from the late medieval period with the compilation of urban 'Bills of Mortality', contemporary interest in population developments led by 1800 to quite widespread official counts of burials, baptisms and marriages. The collected data on the Nordic countries is generally of high quality but the French system largely broke down after the Revolution and remained suspect to the end of our period. Information was assembled by Rickman at the 1801 British census and extended, for England and Wales, at subsequent censuses up to 1841, but the English information is of little real use to the historical demographer [10], and the Scottish material was recognised as almost worthless at the time [11].

Historical demographers have therefore recently returned to the parish registers and instigated new series of counts. For Scotland, the fragmentary registers of over one hundred parishes have been used to construct a rough index of mortality fluctuations [11]. For France, there is an excellent scheme to analyse a representative sample from the parish registers of 413 places in mainland France for the period 1740–1829 [22]. For England the Cambridge Group has estimated national totals of births, deaths and marriages from a sample of 404 high-quality Anglican parish registers [7].

The Cambridge study is a path-breaking one but questions have been raised about sample quality and about the assumptions and techniques used in the analysis [e.g. 55; 54]. The sample is unevenly spread over the country, is skewed towards larger parishes, and excludes London; as a result, major (though superficially reasonable) adjustments have had to be made to the data. Beyond this, as we have seen above, allowance is required for those births, burials and marriages which left no record in the Anglican registers. The cumulative impact of the adjustments for non-representativeness and for non-recording is very large indeed. For example, the number of baptisms *recorded* in the 404 parishes rose by 40 per cent between 1750 and 1800. However, after adjustment for gaps in registration, parish size bias, and the omission of London, the estimated *national total* of Anglican baptisms rose by only 33 per cent; after correction for nonconformity, birth-baptism interval change, and residual non-registration, the *estimated rise in births* is

58 per cent. Some other adjustments, notably for marriages between 1800 and 1837, produce even larger differences. However reasonable the adjustments may be, the end results are only as good as the assumptions made, and a considerable margin of error must be assumed [see especially 55].

Wrigley and Schofield, however, go beyond the raw totals of events. For some years demographers have been experimenting with procedures for deriving population numbers (and also rates of mortality, fertility and nuptiality) from totals of births, deaths and marriages. Wrigley and Schofield's procedure, 'back projection' [7], a development of the 'inverse projection' technique invented by Lee (*Population Studies*, 1974), is based on a simple idea: if one starts from a known census population, then, subtracting the number of births from the previous year and adding the number of deaths gives an estimate of the population at the start of that year. In a world with no emigration, cumulating this process would produce estimated populations backwards, on an annual basis, as far as the beginning of the records of births and deaths.

Unfortunately, because we cannot ignore emigration, a more complex computer-based solution must be employed. It exploits a general demographic observation: regardless of the *level* of mortality, fertility, nuptiality and migration in any year, the *shares* of events between different age groups tend to vary in highly predictable ways. Making suitable assumptions about these shares allows us to proceed as follows: Take the number of persons alive and aged, say, 10–14 at the 1871 census. Then, from the total of deaths between 1866 and 1871, and the assumed age distribution of those deaths, we can estimate the number of deaths of children who had been aged 5–9 in 1866. Adding these dead children to the numbers alive aged 10–14 in 1871 gives a figure for the number of children aged 5–9 in 1866. Repeat this procedure for 1861–6 for children aged 0–4 in 1861; this gives an estimate of the number of 0–4 year olds alive in 1861. A similar procedure can be used across all other age groups. The same procedure for earlier years builds population estimates back in time.

There are, however, two complications. Firstly, the method gives no estimate of the numbers alive in the oldest age group in 1866, the oldest two age groups in 1861, and so on; this is because all members of this age group are assumed to have died by 1871. For each year, therefore, we must estimate the number of very old persons alive so that they can be fed into the 'top' of the model and gradually work their way back to their births. The solution adopted by Wrigley and Schofield is based on the numbers originally born into any age cohort and the mortality experience of the whole society over the lifetime of that cohort; this clearly makes a number of assumptions, but these are not especially problematic for scholars of the 1750–1850 period since the population age structure can be checked back in censuses as far as 1821.

The second complication deals with migration. When any cohort is followed back to age 0–4, the next preceding five-year period will be that during which its members were born. If one adds to the numbers computed as alive at 0–4 at any date the estimated deaths of their age peers during the five years before that date, one gets the numbers who 'should' have been born during the preceding five years. The difference between this figure and the numbers actually 'known' to have been born indicates the extent of emigration by members of the cohort over their lives. Using a standard distribution of the ages at emigration, the migrants can be added to the numbers estimated as alive at the different periods of the cohort's life; the computer program then makes adjustments and produces new estimates of numbers alive and dying in each age group in each year.

The results give both population totals and age estimates. These are a dramatic advance on anything previously achieved, though only as good as the assumptions made in calculating the original numbers of demographic events, and those made by the model. Wrigley and Schofield describe their work as a 'reconstruction' of the population of England and stress the inevitably approximate status of the results. Some scholars have been highly critical of what one has called 'a sand of mere assumption and historical speculation' [Razzell, *New Society*, 1981] but this is unfair; all historical knowledge is reconstruction based on judgements about the extent and direction of bias in surviving records, and on historians' interpretations of their meaning and significance. Certainly, as we have seen, some of the judgements used are open to question, but this is true of all assessments of historical data.

More significantly, Lee (*Population Studies*, 1985) has challenged certain aspects of the logical status of the model (though for our period, his alternative calculations using 'inverse projection' produce very similar results). This, however, illustrates a vital point. In

19

3 Population Change 1750–1850

In 1750 the population of north-west Europe was between 60 and 64 million; by 1850 it was around 116 million. As Table I and Figure 1 show, this dramatic expansion, unprecedented since the sixteenth century, was not evenly spread across the continent. At one extreme, Finland's population almost quadrupled in this period and, before its collapse in the famine of the late 1840s, Ireland's probably grew over three and a half times. At the other extreme was France (and probably Switzerland and the Netherlands); France in 1750 had two-fifths of the population of our area, but her population seems to have grown by less than 50 per cent to 1850, reducing her share to three-tenths of the total. Between the extremes, the population of England and Wales expanded 2.9 times, from about 6.1 million in 1750 to 17.9 million in 1851.

Some of the figures used here involve substantial revisions of earlier estimates. The English population data from Wrigley and Schofield's back projection exercise [7] have modified considerably figures based on Rickman's parish register summaries [see 10]; they show in particular slower growth in the 1760s, but faster growth to the end of the century. Allowance has also been made for under-recording at the early censuses and this raises the early-nineteenth-century figures somewhat.

For Ireland, the problems are greater. Kenneth Connell, the pioneer of Irish demographic history, accepted the censuses of 1821, 1831 and 1841 as the best estimates available for the period [12]; recently, some scholars have suggested substantial under-enumeration at the 1821, 1841 and (by inference) 1851 censuses, though they have been happier with 1831. Other writers have suggested over-enumeration in 1831 and have used the remaining figures relatively unchanged. There is at present no obvious resolution to this debate [a useful summary is in 13]. The figures used here accept the 1831 data and assume that the other censuses were as deficient as the English enumerations of the same dates (probably a conservative assumption); this puts the figures into the mid-band

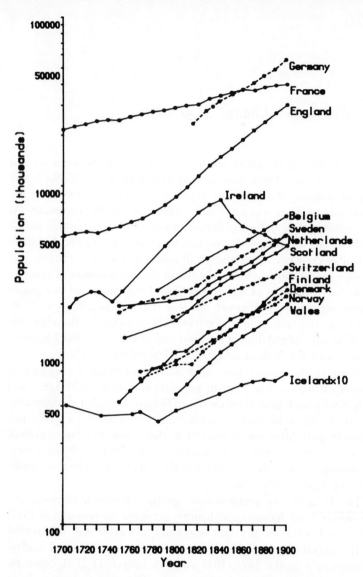

Figure 1 Estimated Populations of Selected Countries, 1700–1900

NOTE

The population figures on the vertical axis are plotted on a logarithmic scale. The effect of this is to ensure that population changes of the same *relative* magnitude produce similar vertical variation on the graph regardless of the initial absolute values. Population growth at a constant rate will produce a straight line

Table I

Estimated Populations of North and West European Countries, c.1750–c.1850 (millions)

	c.1750	c.1800	c.1850
Norway	[0.7]	0.9	1.4
Sweden	1.8	2.3	3.5
Finland	0.5	1.0	1.6
Denmark	[0.7]	0.9	1.4
Iceland	0.0	0.0	0.1
Germany	[18.4]	(24.5)	(35.0)
Netherlands	[1.9]	(2.1)	3.1
Belgium	[2.2]	[2.8]	(4.4)
Switzerland	(1.4)	(1.7)	2.4
France	24.5	29.0	35.9
Scotland	1.3	1.6	2.9
Wales	[0.3]	0.6	1.2
England	5.8	8.7	16.7
Ireland	2.4	[5.2]	6.7
Total	61.9	81.3	116.3

Notes: The figures for Germany are for the 1914 boundaries less Alsace and Lorraine.

The figures for other countries are for the borders of 1850.

Figures in square brackets are very approximate, usually based to some degree on long-term extrapolation or analogy.

Figures in round brackets are based on interpolation between two reasonably sound figures.

For details of the sources and bases of the estimates for France, Ireland, Scotland and England see text. The remaining figures are from B. R. Mitchell, *European Historical Statistics* (1980), modified where appropriate in the light of data or discussions in [4; 16; 17; 19; 21; 25; 26].

of the range of recent estimates.

There is even greater debate over Ireland's population before 1821. The main sources are estimates of the numbers of houses derived from the collection of hearth tax. Contemporaries believed that the pre-1790 figures were too low through laziness, ignorance and corruption of the collectors; recent research tends to ignore the figures between 1753 and 1791 altogether. Connell assumed that the earlier figures were as at least as bad as those of the 1780s; he suggested inflation factors of 50 per cent for 1725 and 1753, and

20 per cent for 1791 [12]. Recent work has been less pessimistic, with under-recording estimated at between 14 per cent and 34 per cent for the earlier years and between 10 per cent and 20 per cent for 1791 ([14a]; Daultry *et al*, *Journal of Economic History*, 1981).

There is also debate for Ireland for this period over the appropriate multiplier to convert houses to people. Connell assumed average household sizes rising from 5.25 to 5.65 between 1725 and 1791 [12]. Detailed research by Daultry and his colleagues suggests a figure of around 5 for 1725 and 1753 but 4.7 for 1744 and 5.8 for 1791 [and see 14a]. The figures used here are from the middle of Daultry's range of estimates and produce a markedly lower 1753 population than Connell's (2.385 million compared with Connell's 3.191). In consequence, growth between 1753 and 1791 is much faster than Connell estimated and growth between 1791 and 1821 is slower, which fits with much contemporary comment suggesting a decline in growth even before the Famine (see also [47; 13]).

Finally, major modifications have recently been made to earlier estimates for France as a result of analysis of the relationship between inter-censal growth on the one hand and the difference between recorded births and recorded deaths on the other [22; 23]. As a result, French population is now believed to have been significantly higher in the mid-eighteenth century than earlier scholars assumed (around 25 million in 1750 as opposed to 21 million); the pace of growth after 1750 is thus even slower than was once thought.

In spite of the tentative nature of the figures, some general statements about the course of population movements can be made. The forty years after 1750 saw most populations growing slowly, typically on a long-run growth rate of around 0.5 per cent per annum but with some setbacks (Swedish population fell, for example, by around 75,000 in the famine of 1772–3). If recent estimates are correct, however, the populations of Ireland and Finland were on a faster growth trajectory, Ireland growing between 1753 and 1791 at 1.7 per cent per annum, Finland on a fluctuating path of around 1.5 per cent per annum until the setback of 1788–90. England's population, though growing at around 0.5 per cent per year in the 1750s and 1760s, thereafter accelerated to exceed 1 per cent by the 1790s.

The Napoleonic war years saw major checks to European population growth. France lost perhaps 1.3 million men [22] as a result of the military campaigns. The wars with Russia brought epidemic and hunger to Sweden, Norway and Finland, with years of absolute decline between 1806–10 and almost no growth for a decade. Only the British Isles escaped, with Ireland, Scotland, and England and Wales experiencing medium-term growth at over 1 per cent per year.

The end of the war saw rapid growth almost everywhere. By 1820 every country in our area had growth approaching, or above, 1 per cent per year; Germany, England and Wales, Ireland, and Norway all approached or exceeded, for at least a decade, the extremely high level of 1.5 per cent per annum; at this rate of growth populations double in fifty years.

Thereafter, growth fell back in most countries. In the 1830s only Germany, England, Norway and Scotland reached 1 per cent per annum growth, while Ireland, Finland and France were probably below 0.5 per cent. The 1840s saw slight recovery in some of the smaller countries, but growth rates in England and Germany continued to fall slowly, and French growth remained very low, at well under 0.5 per cent. Ireland, where the population expansion was already decelerating, experienced a demographic disaster, as the failure of the staple food supply, the potato, led to massive death and emigration. The official census figures, which had been 8.125 million in 1841, fell to 6.552 million in 1851, and then fell further at each census until the 1930s. Elsewhere, excepting Denmark (where population had been sluggish in the early part of the century), and briefly Finland, rates of medium-term growth never again attained the peaks of the years after the Napoleonic wars. Europe was entering a new demographic regime.

These patterns of rise and fall were not spread evenly across the individual territories. Few even among the rural areas significantly lost population before 1800 and only the more isolated regions saw major declines much before 1850. But almost everywhere some areas grew much faster than others. In England the south-east and the industrialising areas of the north rapidly outstripped the remainder of the country, while in Scotland the central belt expanded its population share, mainly at the expense of the highland north. In Sweden, the north and west grew much faster than the east. In Switzerland the Alpine areas grew most slowly. In Germany in the first half of the nineteenth century, growth was high in the agricultural east, moderate in the industrialising west and low in the south. Similar variations occurred elsewhere.

In some countries considerable growth took place in rural areas (particularly areas of rural industrialisation), but increasingly the urban areas were the most dynamic sectors, in spite of their high levels of mortality. One estimate [5] suggests that in 1750 north-western Europe had 160 cities of at least 10,000 people, and a total city population of 4.4 million, some 7 per cent of the total. Using 10,000 population as our minimum size definition, in 1750 only the Netherlands had more than 30 per cent of its population urbanised; Belgium had around 20 per cent, England and Wales about 17 per cent. Nowhere else except Denmark exceeded 10 per cent, and Ireland, Switzerland and the rest of Scandinavia had less than 5 per cent.

By 1800 urban growth was widespread; there were 240 places of over 10,000 people in 1800, and the urban population exceeded 7.5 million. By 1850 the number of cities had risen to 552, with a population of over 20 million, 17 per cent of the total. Over two-fifths of the population of England and Wales lived in cities of over 10,000 people, as did one in three of the people of Scotland and the Netherlands, and one-fifth of all Belgians. By contrast, the figures for France were 15 per cent, for Germany 11 per cent, Ireland 10 per cent, and for the Nordic countries an average of only 6 per cent.

4   *Migration*

There are two ways in which a population can grow: from an excess of births over deaths; and from an excess of immigrants over emigrants. In Europe in our period the first was much more important than the second.

Internal migration, however, played a vital part in the rapid growth of cities, where deaths usually exceeded births until well into our period, and areas of rural industrial expansion were also highly dependent on immigrants. There were also some regions, particularly in the north and east, where pioneers were still moving in and establishing new areas of settlement. Nationally, however, the net direct effect on populations of most of these internal shufflings of people was zero though some inter-state migration, especially within the British Isles, and in the north and east of the continent, must have produced some now largely unmeasurable effects on national population totals.

Overseas movements, by contrast, have at certain periods in the past produced important net effects on national populations; in the fifty years before the First World War Europe permanently lost well over 20 million people to other regions of the world. In our period, however, few movements were, even relatively, on anything like this scale.

In France, small-scale immigration (especially of industrial workers) offset low emigration, leaving little net change except for deaths overseas of soldiers of the French armies during the Napoleonic wars (this was also a problem for the Swiss who, until the 1830s, provided major mercenary contingents to the armies of continental Europe). In England total net loss in any decade probably never rose above 1.5 per thousand of the population, and much of this 'emigration' was due to deaths of soldiers and sailors overseas. In Scotland, besides a flow to England of unknown proportions (until the 1840s when it was about 75,000 net for the decade as a whole), there were recurrent waves of overseas migration; none, however, is likely to have exceeded proportionally that of the 1770s which involved less than 2 per cent of the population at a time when population growth may have been approaching 1 per cent per annum. In the Nordic countries legal restrictions on emigration in the eighteenth century meant that most of those who left did so clandestinely and precise figures are lacking. Except for some small movements to Finland in the eighteenth century, however, Swedish emigration was probably insignificant until the lifting of last major restrictions in the 1840s when a considerable outflow began. In Norway emigration was low with even the peak loss, for the period 1845–50, being a mere 0.3 per cent of the 1845 population. Emigration from Denmark was equally trivial.

Elsewhere, emigration was more significant, especially in Switzerland and Germany, and particularly following the potato harvest failures of 1816–17 and 1847; in the late 1840s over 300,000 Germans emigrated, from a population of just over 30 million. But Ireland had the most dramatic population outflows. About 1.75 million people emigrated between 1780 and 1844, perhaps two-fifths to Great Britain, the rest mainly to North America; this held back population growth to around three-quarters of natural increase between 1780 and 1844. Yet this was insignificant compared with what followed. During and immediately after the famine of 1845–8, at least one million people left, around one-eighth of the 1841 population. Nowhere else in our period did emigration have this impact. Everywhere else it was the balance between births and deaths which was the main mechanism of population growth or decline.

5   Natural Increase

'Natural increase' (normally computed per thousand of the population so as to allow easy comparison between populations of different sizes) is calculated by taking the difference between the 'crude birth rate' of a population and its 'crude death rate'. The 'crude birth rate' is the number of births in any year in an area, divided by the population and multiplied by 1000. The 'crude death rate' is computed in a similar way. At times, both these indicators can be misleading or inadequate, particularly during periods of rapid demographic growth when population age structures become skewed towards younger age groups. Crude rates nevertheless provide useful and widely available clues about the relative importance of fertilty and mortality in overall population change.

Figure 2 sets the crude rates of our period in a longer term context for countries with precise enough information to reveal trends over a reasonable period of time. However, even these figures are often only approximate, certainly before the 1820s. For example, the Norwegian statistics used here are taken from Drake's work [21] and make rather different assumptions from those of earlier scholars [e.g. 15] about stillbirths and about the accuracy of the 1769 census. Wrigley and Schofield's figures for England [7] are subject to limitations arising from their method of estimation, and their conclusions are still disputed by some scholars who believe that the early-nineteenth-century birth rates and the later-eighteenth-century death rates are both too high [e.g. 55; 58].

Looking first at the birth rate trends as plotted in Figure 2, the most striking feature is the differences in the levels and trends between countries. Comparing the figures, one pattern occurs in England where the birth rate was around 34 per 1000 in the 1750s, then rose, particularly from the 1780s, to over 40 by 1820, followed by a fairly rapid fall to roughly mid-eighteenth-century levels. In complete contrast was the situation of France (which differed, indeed, from any other country). The mid-eighteenth-century birth rate, at around 40 per 1000, was exceeded only by that of Finland.

29

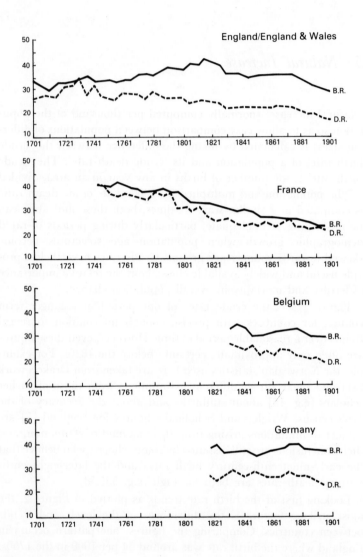

Figure 2 Crude Birth and Crude Death Rates (per 1000 population), Selected Countries, 1701–1901

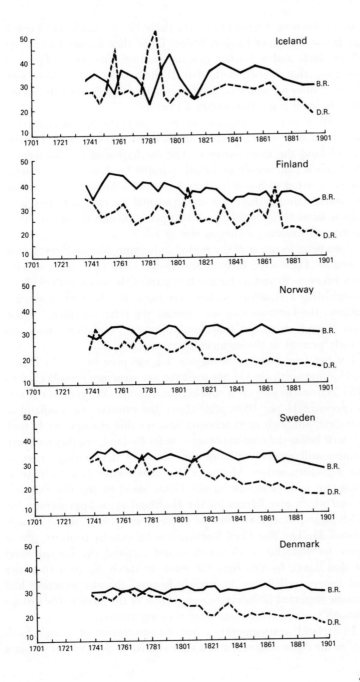

31

A slight downward tendency by the early 1790s brought the French rate below the rising English figure. There then followed a sharper fall by 1800 and a further gradual decline after 1820. The end result was that France in the late 1840s had the lowest birth rate of any country for which we have reasonable figures, the rate having fallen by over a quarter within a century.

Equally dramatic contrasts can be found in the Nordic countries, though all five countries show marked fluctuations, with Iceland and Finland the most extreme. The oscillation of the Norwegian birth rate is commented on below; parallel but less extreme fluctuations occurred in Sweden (though around a higher trend) and in Denmark, though there the quinquennial average rate lies in a narrow band between 29.0 and 32.5 per 1000 and the trend shows no marked tendency either to rise or fall.

Elsewhere, for most of the period only impressionistic results are available. The Swiss, Belgian and Dutch birth rates seem to have been between 30 and 35 for the first part of the nineteenth century, though with a tendency to fall over time. By the mid-nineteenth century, the German rate was around the relatively high English level, though there was considerable internal variation which was already present in the eighteenth century [4c].

For Scotland (where the figures are too poor to plot in Figure 2), Hollingsworth [in 11] has used the age structure from Webster's 1755 'census' to suggest a mid-eighteenth-century crude birth rate in excess of 41 per 1000, well above the estimate for England at that date; although most scholars now see this as implausibly high it is well below the contemporary rate for Finland, another northern country still recovering from the effects of devastating crises of half a century earlier. Moreover, Hollingsworth's 1755 estimate is consistent with estimates for the 1790s based on the *Old Statistical Account* which give figures for the Highland areas approaching the 1750s figure, though for the rest of the country the estimate is only around 35. The first Civil Registration figures, by contrast, give a figure for 1855–60 of 34 per thousand (around the English level for that date); by this time the most northerly Scottish countries had figures well below 30, mainly because the age structure had become distorted by heavy out-migration of the most fertile groups (though low marriage rates were also important).

In Ireland, contemporaries had an impression of a high birth rate in the eighteenth century, a view shared by most recent scholars [reviewed in 13]. The 1841 census, however, estimated a rate of only 33 per 1000, implying a fall since 1800; this figure, though widely cited, is based on the published census information on ages of infants, and this must be faulty. Had the birth rate been this low, the Irish death rate in the twenty years before the famine (at 17 per 1000) would have been the lowest in Europe, which seems very unlikely. Mokyr [47], using plausible though sweeping assumptions, has proposed a birth rate of around 40 per thousand for the years 1821–40. This, however, unreasonably implies a death rate worse than any Nordic country except Finland and is thus surely too high; nevertheless, throughout our period and certainly right up to the eve of the Famine, Ireland's fertility was at the high end of the European spectrum.

Turning now to death rates, three features are particularly striking: the wide differences in rates in the mid-eighteenth century, the tendency for most rates to fall significantly by the mid-nineteenth century (though often on rather different timings and trajectories), and the continuing fluctuations apparent in some countries even when five or ten year averages are taken. While all these aspects are clearly visible at the national levels shown in Figure 2, they are even more apparent at local and regional levels, a point which is further discussed below.

The first half of the eighteenth century saw mortality in most countries as higher than in the second half. Wrigley and Schofield's estimate [7] puts the average English crude death rate at over 31 per 1000 population for the years 1720–45, but only at around 27 per 1000 for the next 40 years; note also the relatively small amplitude of the English death rate fluctuations. Scandinavia experienced severe problems in the 1740s, with the Finnish, Icelandic and Swedish death rates over 40 in at least one year and the Norwegian exceeding 70 per 1000 in 1742. Thereafter, for the rest of the century, the Swedish and Norwegian rates fluctuated around an average level similar to the English; the Danish average was a little higher but more stable, while the Finnish and Icelandic rates fluctuated considerably but still on a medium-term trend well below 30 per 1000 [15–17].

Elsewhere, the situation in France in the mid-eighteenth century was bad; recent estimates suggest a death rate of around 40 per 1000 population in the 1740s and around 35 for the next forty years [22; 23]. In many parts of Germany, by contrast, the eighteenth-century death rate hovered around or above 30 [4c] and one interpretation of the fragmentary Scottish materials suggests a death rate for the years before 1755 of well over 35 per 1000, but a fall to below 30 by the 1790s, with rates for rural areas of below 25 [11]. Finally, for Ireland, no hard information is available and, though most demographers assume a death rate fairly well in check, there is ongoing debate over the severity of the several regional crises which clearly did occur (summary in [13]).

As is clear from Figure 2, when compared with the mid-eighteenth century, the death rates of the 1820s were almost everywhere more favourable. English mortality had fallen significantly over the previous forty years, to a medium-term trend around 22 per thousand; there it remained until well after the end of our period, though possibly rising a little in the 1840s as a result of the massive urbanisation of the previous thirty years. Scottish death rates in the 1850s were somewhat below the English levels, but Scottish mortality, particularly in the towns, may also have shifted upwards in the 1930s and 1840s. Mokyr's [47] recent estimate for Ireland for 1821–41 gives a national figure of around 24 per 1000, though he suggests that Ulster may have recorded a rate of less than 22; the argument that implies that this was below the eighteenth-century level is, however, based largely on impression (and see [6]). In the Famine years of the late 1840s the Irish situation was transformed. The number of excess deaths during these years was between one and one and a half million, producing a national death rate for the period of over 50 per 1000 [47].

On the Continent, the most dramatic changes were taking place in France. Around the turn of the century the death rate stepped down quite sharply to around 30 per 1000; it fell further before the end of the Napoleonic Wars and by the 1840s was not far above the English level. Scandinavian rates also moved downwards by the early nineteenth century, though the Nordic area was severely hit in 1808–9, and in Finland and Iceland occasional surges of mortality continued for much of the rest of the century. Nevertheless, by the end of our period Denmark, Norway and Sweden were on trend averages between 18 and 21 per 1000 population. This was in clear contrast with the lands to the south, where Germany and the Low Countries persisted with death rates only marginally below those of the late eighteenth century.

The net results of these changes in medium-term death and birth rates can be seen in the rates of natural increase, revealed by the gaps between the birth and death rate lines in Figure 2. As we have seen earlier, population grew markedly between 1750 and 1850 almost right across the continent and it increased particularly fast in the years after the Napoleonic wars. Everywhere, most of this growth came from natural increase. However, as the graphs make clear, the ways in which this natural increase was achieved varied considerably between different parts of our area.

One pattern is clearly visible in Norway, Sweden, and with slight modifications, in Denmark. In these countries, natural increase was at moderate levels in the eighteenth century and the acceleration in population growth came largely from a gradual fall in the death rate against a stable or more slowly falling birth rate; the temporary very rapid growth around 1820 was the result of a trough in the death rate coinciding with a brief surge in births.

The English pattern seems very different. A falling death rate helped to accelerate population growth in the second half of the eighteenth century, but the rising birth rate was clearly the more volatile component; in particular, the timing of the peak growth in the 1810s, and its subsequent decline to around the average Euro-pean level, were mainly determined by birth rate changes. The relative importance of the birth and death rate components depends on the dates chosen for comparison. Wrigley and Schofield [7] suggest that around three-quarters of the rise in growth between the mid-seventeenth and early nineteenth centuries resulted from the birth rate side of the equation. Thus, in most modern interpret-ations, fertility is seen as the dominant partner; the older, and once dominant, view [e.g. 10; 42] that fertility could not possibly have been dynamic enough to play more than a minor role, is now clearly on the defensive.

France offers a third and apparently unique growth profile, where a falling death rate fails to produce more than short-term bursts of growth because of compensating and only slightly lagged falls in fertility.

Fourthly, there is Finland, where an extremely high birth rate, particularly in the eighteenth century, moved against a slowly falling underlying death rate. This produced rapid medium-term growth in spite of occasional dramatic mortality crises, a pattern which continued to the end of the nineteenth century. Possible parallels with Ireland are suggestive. One may also wonder whether

35

parts of eighteenth-century Scotland might not have been on a similar trajectory, only being saved from the fate of Ireland and Finland by the arrival in the later eighteenth century of radically improved poor relief administration, agrarian reform and industrialisation. Iceland may also fit this pattern, though the recurrent mortality crises, and their reverberations on the birth rate, were even more severe and frequent, so that long-run growth was more controlled.

Finally, we should note that nineteenth-century Germany, with its continuing high birth and death rates, looks very different from the rest of our area.

Ten years ago, historical demographers still felt reasonably happy in extrapolating from the experience of one Western European country to another (a view exemplified by Flinn [3]). We can no longer safely think in these terms. While overall growth patterns clearly show some similarities, the factors underlying them were very different. The next sections seek to identify the causes of these different profiles of growth.

6 Fertility and Nuptiality

The previous section has shown that variations in birth rates were an important mechanism of demographic change. We can distinguish four factors which may help in understanding these variations: compositional effects, illegitimacy and pre-nuptial pregnancy, changes in marital fertility, and changes in marriage patterns.

(i) COMPOSITIONAL EFFECTS

Compositional effects operate on crude birth rates when there are sharp variations in the proportions of populations who are females in the fertile age groups. The oscillations in the Norwegian birth rate (see Figure 2) provide a classic example, first noted by Sundt in the 1850s [79; and see 21]. Sundt argued that the crisis of the 1740s reduced fertility and also killed many children. As a result, a small age cohort entered marriage around 1770 and births fell by an eighth in ten years. When the larger cohort born in the 1760s married in the 1780s, the number of births rose again; the small 1770s cohort, by contrast, produced a 10 per cent reduction in births by 1806–10. Further fluctuations continued to the 1830s. As Sundt acknowledged, other factors were also involved; heavy taxation in the 1760s and the dearths of the 1770s played a part, while 1806–10 saw disruptive warfare. Nevertheless, the compositional factor is a major component of the cyclical changes in Norway's crude birth rates, and it influenced even the surge and slump of births which contributed to the rapid population expansion of the 1820s and the slower growth which followed it.

Oscillations in Iceland had partly similar origins, as, on a smaller scale, they did also in Sweden, Denmark and Finland. Elsewhere, however, while small variations in birth rates may have resulted from changes in population age composition, the effects were much less important.

Between 1740 and 1790, the proportion of births which occurred outside marriage rose almost everywhere [91; 92; Tomasson, *Comparative Studies in Society and History*, 1976]. In England the percentage of all births which were illegitimate (the 'illegitimacy ratio') was about 3 per cent around 1750, about 5 per cent by 1800 and 6.5 per cent by 1850. In France, the figures were initially lower (probably around 1.5 per cent in the 1750s), but they rose slowly until the 1780s, then sharply to 5.5 per cent by the 1820s and to over 7 per cent by 1850. In Sweden, illegitimate births rose very fast, from around 2 per cent of births about 1750 to 6 per cent around 1800 and 9 per cent by the mid-nineteenth century. In other Nordic countries there were broadly parallel rises; the illegitimacy ratio for the 1850s reached 14.3 per cent in Iceland, 11.1 per cent in Denmark, 8.7 per cent in Norway and 7.0 per cent in Finland. There were also rises in Scotland (probably mainly in the nineteenth century), and in most parts of Germany, where the figure for many parishes exceeded 10 per cent by the end of our period. Only in Ireland does illegitimacy seem always to have been low, perhaps one birth in forty even just before the Famine, but the fragmentary nature of the evidence cautions against too dogmatic assertion of this point.

These changes are interesting for students of social structure, but their demographic importance is minor. In England between 1750 and 1816, for example, only about 10 per cent of the rise in all births is attributable to the increase in illegitimacy. In France, the near quadrupling of illegitimacy between the 1750s and the 1820s offset only about one-eighth of the fall in legitimate births; in Sweden the increased illegitimacy offset at most one-third of the fall in legitimate births over the period.

These are the direct effects. Is it possible that rising illegitimacy (and the increasing pre-nuptial conceptions that generally accompanied it) encouraged women into earlier marriages than would otherwise have occurred, thus exposing them to lengthier marriages and consequential higher fertility? Since around half of all first births in England in the early nineteenth century were probably conceived outside wedlock, this effect could in theory have been important. In practice, however, most women who conceived outside marriage were of roughly similar ages to those conceiving their first babies inside marriage; most pre-marital conceptions probably therefore involved couples anticipating the date of ecclesiastical union, often perhaps, following local lay custom as to when a betrothed couple could legitimately commence sexual relations [7; 91]. Overall, variations in rates of pre-nuptial and extra-marital pregnancy explain little of the overall changes in population growth rates in our period.

(iii)   VARIATIONS IN MARITAL FERTILITY

When the birth rate fell in Western Europe in the last quarter of the nineteenth century, a decline in married women's fertility was the major cause. How important was change in the birth rate in our period?

Table II shows 'age-specific marital fertility rates' and 'total marital fertility ratios' for various parts of our area. Age-specific marital fertility rates are calculated for any five-year age group by the following formula:

$$\frac{\text{number of births experienced by married women in an age group} \times 1000}{\text{number of years lived by married women in that age group}}$$

Thus, if a group of women aged 25–29 lived in total for 400 years in the married state, and experienced in that period 120 births, the age-specific marital fertility rate for this age group would be:

$$\frac{120}{400} \times 1000 = 300$$

The 'total marital fertility ratio' (TMFR), is a derivation from the age-specific marital fertility rate. As used here, it shows, for any area, the number of children who would have been born to a woman who married in that area at age 20, and who experienced the area's average age-specific marital fertility rates between the ages of 20 and 44. This is not the same as average family size (that would be influenced by the proportion of women married in the different age groups); instead, TMFR provides a standard way of comparing, in a single figure, the fertility component of the marital fertility experience of different communities or countries over time.

Apart from Scandinavia, most of the figures in Table II are from

Table II
Age-specific Marital Fertility Rates and Total Marital Fertility Ratios (TMFR) (ages 20–44) for Selected Countries and Regions

Area		Marital fertility rates					
		20–24	25–29	30–34	35–39	40–44	TMFR
England 13 parishes	1700–49	415	364	306	238	126	7.25
	1750–99	423	356	289	237	133	7.19
Scotland national	1855	427	366	302	242	113	7.25
Sweden national	1751–80	455	381	330	232	126	7.62
	1781–1820	461	355	322	225	145	7.54
	1821–50	463	372	318	242	136	7.67
Germany 14 villages	1750–74	439	425	374	303	173	8.57
	1800–24	463	412	362	285	151	8.37
	1850–74	533	450	362	258	128	8.80
Denmark national	1760–1801	495	415	358	326	181	8.88
Belgium 6 parishes	later 18C	494	476	385	313	204	9.36
end 18/C	early 19C	543	464	433	329	178	9.75
France (NW) 10 parishes	1740–69	455	415	379	285	130	8.32
	1770–89	465	406	362	273	117	8.12
	1790–1819	444	366	288	189	74	6.81
(NE) 12 parishes	1740–69	486	444	396	326	149	9.00
	1770–89	488	481	425	296	131	9.11
	1790–1819	426	367	317	243	95	7.24
(SW) 9 parishes	1740–69	407	374	349	267	142	7.70
	1770–89	413	350	323	253	132	7.36
	1790–1819	381	353	312	238	99	6.92
(SE) 10 parishes	1740–69	389	393	370	286	140	7.89
	1770–89	398	382	352	274	138	7.72
	1780–1819	398	369	312	247	111	7.19

Note: The French figures are calculated as the means of the figures for the separate age-at-marriage groups and are therefore approximate and are probably slight underestimates, especially for the early years. Because the data were not published in a totally standard form there are also some minor inconsistencies between the different regions of the country.

The German figures are from Knodel's paper in [69]. Part of the increase among young women is attributable to rising pre-nuptial pregnancy. This is probably also a factor elsewhere.

The remaining figures are from [3; 9; 11; 17; 72–75].

family reconstitutions of a relatively small number of parishes. In France they are based on systematic sampling of rural areas [22], but the English figures are from a rather arbitrary collection of places [9].

Note first in Table II the major differences between countries in the eighteenth century. In most areas, total marital fertility ratios lay between around 8 and 9.5, but in England and, to some extent, Sweden, the figures were lower. The age-specific marital fertility figures show that this lower overall fertility is reflected in lower fertility at all ages, a point to which we shall return.

Secondly, there were significant differences in the patterns of internal variation within countries. In particular, England differed from most of the continent in the similarity of its figures across parishes. In one study of 14 parishes [70], no parish produced a total marital fertility ratio above 8.0 and, though two lie around 6.0, most cluster close to the average value. By contrast, there were substantial variations between different Swedish and Finnish parishes, larger than would result from random variation. And in France during the eighteenth century there were marked regional variations ([72–75; 23] and see Table II); completed family size of women marrying between the ages of 25 and 29 in the period 1720–39 ranged between 6.4 in the north-east quarter of the country and 5.2 in the south-west. In our period, as Table II shows, variations in age-specific and in total marital fertility continued, with the north-east by 1770–89 having a total marital fertility ratio nearly two children higher than the south-west. Women marrying at 25–29 had estimated average completed family sizes of 5.5 in the north-east, and 4.8 in the south-west.

A third feature of the changes in marital fertility patterns in our period is their different paths over time. In England, marital fertility appears remarkably constant between 1600 and 1800; the total marital fertility ratios for the four half-centuries between these two dates all lie between 7.19 and 7.27. The picture after 1800 is obscure in the absence of adequate numbers of reliable reconstitutions; this is particularly unfortunate given the birth rate surge of this period. By 1851 marital fertility was still around the late-eighteenth-century level, but the possibility remains that a temporary rise had played some role in the rapid population growth of the previous fifty years. On present evidence, however, changes in marital fertility were not important in English population changes in our period.

By contrast, in France, falls in marital fertility began at an early date. In most areas, completed family size of women who married between 25 and 29 was nearly one child lower in the years 1770–89 than it had been in the 1720s and 1730s. By 1790–1819, a further fall (plus the near disappearance of regional differences) left the north-east at one extreme with completed family size at 4.5 and the south-east at the other with families of 4.2. The total marital fertility ratios shown in Table II reveal the same pattern, with the figures down everywhere, and with the largest falls in the previously highest fertility areas. The falls occurred at almost all ages, but were proportionately largest at the older ages [for details see 72–75; 23].

It should be noted from Table II, however, that even after the falls, the total marital fertility of French women marrying in 1790–1819 was still in most areas only around the level found in England over the previous two hundred years. Controlling for age at marriage, for women marrying in the 25–29 age group, the TMFR for English women for 1600–1799 was 5.54, the same as for north-west France for 1789–1819, and below that for the north-east (5.70). Only among women marrying in the last thirty years of our period, as fertility fell still further, did France as a whole have uniquely small family sizes.

How can we explain these considerable variations in fertility levels and the changes which occurred, particularly in France, before the end of our period? Three aspects merit attention: 'fecundability' and 'fecundity', infant mortality, and conscious fertility limitation.

'Fecundability' comprises the set of factors which affect the likelihood that a woman will bear children if she is regularly exposed to intercourse and takes no steps to prevent conception. They include some which could have been relevant but which are impossible to research rigorously with the data available for our period (for example, effects of changes in health and nutrition on frequency of intercourse, declines in periods of separation of spouses, and reduction in stillbirths) [85; for a recent technical review see 69]. Fortunately, none of these seem likely to have varied enough to be very important in our period.

More significant might be changes in 'fecundity' (the physiological ability of women to bear children). Knodel points to a rise in fecundity to explain the increased marital fertility of younger women in his German villages between the mid-eighteenth and later nineteenth century (see Table II and [85]); this suggestion is strengthened by another finding: a shortening gap between marriage and first birth for women who were not pregnant at the time of their marriage. Netting [68] attributes much of the 30 per cent rise in fertility between 1750–99 and 1900–49 in a Swiss mountain village to improved fecundity, and he argues that rises in underlying fecundity were also occurring elsewhere in Switzerland. However, changes in marital fertility at younger ages in Sweden suggest a fall in underlying fecundity over the course of the nineteenth century.

The extent and causes of such changes, however, require further research. Improvements in health might have played some role in some areas. Venereal diseases were probably spreading in towns in the nineteenth century and must have held down fertility, though the size of differentials between countries and periods is unclear. Malaria, which was prevalent in parts of Scandinavia until reduced by drainage in the nineteenth century, and smallpox, which declined at the same period, can also limit fecundity; their control might have increased early-nineteenth-century birth rates. There is also an ingenious suggestion [58] that increasing potato consumption in the eighteenth century reduced exposure to the contraceptive efforts of toxins present in some grain moulds; the argument is, however, highly inferential and seems incompatible with at least some parts of the modern geographical incidence of the fungi.

Other aspects of nutrition have also been invoked to explain variations in fertility. Short-term falls in births, which occurred widely in harvest crisis years, have been linked to this factor, while improved diet has been seen as an explanation of longer term rises in birth rates (as in Switzerland) [68] and of generally high fertility (as in Ireland); in these latter cases a major role has been attributed to the potato, though recent scholarship views the evidence as inconclusive [12; 13]. However, suggestions that have been made that nutrition – or indeed fungi – was important in England seem implausible; as we have seen, English *marital* fertility seems to have been roughly constant over time, a finding inconsistent with improved fecundity unless there were compensating reductions from other causes.

There are, anyway, two problems that the nutrition-fertility explanation has to confront. Firstly, as we shall see below, it is not clear that nutrition levels for the mass of the population did rise markedly over our period; in some areas they fell in the eighteenth century, though *fluctuations* in food supply diminished over time [43; 95]. Secondly, work which identified a mechanism linking critical body weight with temporary sterility has now been challenged on both data and methodological grounds, and recent work on the fecundity of women in modern less developed countries casts doubt on the importance of the nutrition hypothesis [see 69; 39a]. For example, a survey comparing the fertility of the best- and the worst-fed tenths of a sample of women in Bangladesh showed average birth intervals only 10 per cent shorter in the best-fed group. From what little we know of levels of nutrition in Western Europe in our period, it thus seems unlikely that changes and differences in access to food had any major effect on the fertility changes which we have observed earlier in this book.

Attention has instead recently focused on possible effects of variations in breastfeeding practices. Research on fertility in less developed countries suggests that women who do not breastfeed wait on average only two months before their next conception, compared with nearly 18 months for women breastfeeding for two years [69]. For most historical populations, breastfeeding changes remain poorly researched but recent work on England (where breastfeeding was probably the most important factor keeping fertility low) [87], and on Germany [82] and Sweden/Finland [88] is of interest.

Table III shows that the total marital fertility ratio in Nar on the island of Gotland was only about two-thirds of that of Petalax in Finland at roughly the same dates. In Nar breastfeeding was normal and extended for two to three years; in Petalax it was almost unknown [88]. Work on German villages in the mid-nineteenth century shows fertility implications of breastfeeding to the extent that, where lactation was short, total marital fertility ratios reached 10.6 [82].

The most extreme example of this breastfeeding-fertility link, however, was in France; the widespread use of wet nurses (especially among urban populations), and short periods of breastfeeding (revealed by contemporary comment and by the seasonal patterns of infant mortality), were major factors in the high fertility of some areas in the eighteenth century [e.g. van de Walle in 91]. Detailed

Table III
*Age-specific Marital Fertility Rates and Total Marital Fertility Ratios (ages 20–44)
for Selected Places*

Area		Marital fertility rates						
		20–24	25–29	30–34	35–39	40–44	TMFR	m
Sweden, Nar	1830–65	341	391	260	235	97	6.62	0.208
Finland, Petalax	1826–65	596	433	426	387	169	10.06	0.084
	1690–1719	541	568	509	361	160	10.70	0.168
	1740–69	576	504	459	310	140	9.95	0.282
France, Vic-s-Seille	1790–1819	483	412	333	205	96	7.65	0.453
	1700–49	395	368	397	255	112	7.64	0.164
England, Shepshed	1750–1824	447	344	315	256	135	7.49	0.101
Sweden, Alskog	1745–1820	345	337	265	174	90	6.06	0.294
Åsunda	1820–50	337	295	234	182	79	5.64	0.301

Note: The French figures are the means of age-at-marriage-specific data for age groups 15–19, 20–24, 25–29 and 30–34.
The statistic *m* indicates the divergence of an age-specific marital fertility pattern from a 'natural fertility' regime (see page 46) [47].
The data are taken from [63; 67; 74; 80; 88].

research on the Swedish/German model is limited for France but Flandrin [24], in particular, has argued that a rise in breastfeeding contributed significantly to the falls in infant mortality and fertility in the late eighteenth century. Similar arguments may be relevant elsewhere, though for most countries it has not been convincingly demonstrated that the well-documented medical concern over the problem of artificial feeding produced changes in actual behaviour; changes in the age pattern of infant mortality in parts of Sweden would be compatible with this interpretation [43], but apparent continued indifference elsewhere even after the mid-nineteenth century would not [43d; 43g; 86; 52].

Infant mortality declines were widespread in our period and, assuming reasonable periods of lactation, this should also have produced a more direct effect on fertility, though the precise impact of such changes requires further research. It is clear, however, that in France the areas of highest fertility had infant mortality rates at least 50 per cent above those of low fertility areas; as infant mortality fell over the later eighteenth and early nineteenth century so too did fertility; the one exceptional area, Brittany (where fertility rose), also showed an increase in infant deaths [24].

The third possible influence on marital fertility we must consider is deliberate attempts at contraception. Swedish/Finnish and German evidence shows that some women understood the contraceptive effects of prolonged breastfeeding [86; 43d] and, while mechanical techniques were unimportant, in many areas *coitus interruptus* (withdrawal before ejaculation) and abortion were clearly options open to couples who wished to restrict family size [90; 88].

There are, however, few areas where evidence on conscious use of fertility limitation is unambiguous. One such is Vic-sur-Seille, a small town in north-east France where, as can be seen from Table III, marital fertility fell significantly between marriages of the turn of the eighteenth century and marriages one hundred years later [74]. The total marital fertility ratio fell from 10.70 to 7.65, a decline of some 28 per cent; the decline was steady, and is notable because it began even before 1750 and was statistically large enough for random fluctuations to be ruled out as a possible alternative explanation.

How do we know that conscious fertility limitation was involved? Firstly, as Table III shows, it was especially among older women that marital fertility fell; this suggests attempts to 'stop' having further children once a target level had been reached (as happens with most married couples in Western societies today). In a 'natural fertility' regime (where couples make no attempt to control fertility on the basis of the number of previous births) the curve of age-specific fertility falls steadily over a woman's life as her biological fecundity declines (see the curve for the 1670–1719 cohort in Figure 3). By contrast, when older women limit their fertility, the curve tends towards an inverted S-shape, with a steep fall in the middle years of marriage (as in the 1790–1819 curve). A statistic (m) has been developed to indicate the divergence of an age-specific marital fertility pattern from a 'natural fertility' regime. With no fertility limitation the statistic approximates to 0.0, but m values of over 0.2 or 0.3 are taken to indicate limitation. As Table III shows, the m values for Vic-sur-Seille move away from 'natural fertility' at an early date.

Could disease, poor nutrition, a spread of prolonged breastfeeding or even disruption of married life during wartime, have produced the changes in fertility in Vic-sur-Seille? This is unlikely since it is particularly the older women who were affected and the later birth

46

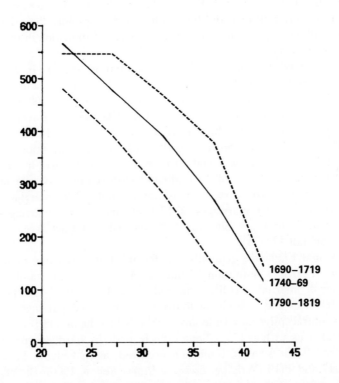

Figure 3 Age-specific Marital Fertility Rates of Women Marrying before Age 25, Vic-sur-Seille, 1670–1719 to 1790–1819

intervals which were prolonged. Of women marrying at ages 20–24 in 1720–69, 27 per cent had had their last child by age 35, but a quarter of women marrying at these ages in 1770–1818 had already stopped by 30. Median ages at the birth of last child fell from 40.5 to 36.7. Moreover, in the last period, younger marrying women had much lower fertility in their thirties than older marrying women. This is compatible with younger marriers having achieved their target family sizes and seeking to limit further births; it also reduces the possibility that the whole cohort was struck by disease

47

or nutritional problems. Finally, the fertility of the literate (and presumably healthier and better off) fell more rapidly than that of their illiterate peers, not the predicted pattern if nutrition or disease were important.

This kind of evidence for fertility limitation appears in certain places in our area for even earlier dates. The Genevan bourgeoisie had total marital fertility ratios around 6.5 soon after 1700; women marrying in their early twenties had their last child on average at age 34; their mean last birth interval was 51 months [71]. Members of the French elite showed equally early fertility limitation (Levy and Henry, *Population*, 1960). In parts of rural France, limitation appears in marriages of the mid-eighteenth century. Average completed family size in rural areas was around 6.2 for marriages of 1720–39, 6.0 for marriages of 1740–69 and 5.6 for marriages of 1770–89. The years following 1789 showed a marked acceleration of this fall [72–75].

Could England's generally low fertility have been due to widespread fertility limitation within marriage? Almost certainly not. English marital fertility changed very little over the period 1600–1799 and a study of fourteen reconstituted parishes shows no contraceptive pattern in any of them when the period 1600–1799 is taken as a whole [70] (though this is, perhaps, hardly surprising). Where some signs of limitation occurred, as in Colyton between 1647 and 1719 (Wrigley, *Economic History Review*, 1966), the effects are not marked, and may even stem from random fluctuations due to the small numbers of events observed. Even for the framework knitting village of Shepshed [63], a careful inspection of the figures in Table III suggests a picture less clear than has been claimed.

Elsewhere in Europe the pattern is variable. A study of fifteen German villages in the century before 1850 shows evidence of limited fertility control before 1800 in only one, with two more showing some restriction among women marrying between 1825 and 1849 [82; 84]. Only in these two latter cases, moreover, is the restriction marked, with m values of 0.34 and 0.37. However, the lowest age at birth of last child for 1825–49 was only 37.9 and the longest average last birth interval 48 months. We may thus conclude that in Germany active birth control was only beginning by 1850; it did not play much role in our period.

By contrast, in Sweden, fertility restriction may have been more important from an earlier date. In Alskog, on Gotland, average completed family size for marriages of 1795–1820 was only 4.3 and the patterns of age-specific marital fertility rate (see Table III) are compatible with deliberate family limitation. Though the low fertility rates of women in their twenties might reflect the extended breastfeeding common in that part of Sweden, the differences between the fertility in their thirties of younger and older marrying women is clearly indicative of a desire to restrict family size (see [80]).

Similar evidence exists for other areas. In Åsunda in east central Sweden in the early nineteenth century age-specific marital fertility was very low at all ages; the total marital fertility ratio was 5.21 for women born in 1804–6 and average completed family size was 4.2. Breastfeeding cannot be the explanation here since the mean age at birth of last child was 36.5 [66]. However, Erisksson and Rogers are tentative about explanations for this low fertility, suggesting that almost total abstinence from intercourse (once desired family size was achieved) may have been common in an area where most marriages were arranged and couples may have had little physical or emotional attraction to each other.

This idea merits further consideration, though it is difficult to research definitively. It is clear that there were other areas (parts of Germany, for example) where deaths of older children in a family increased the subsequent fertility of the parents [83]. This suggests that couples were not reproducing at their biological maximum and that some element of choice was involved. Possibly, interpersonal attitudes changed during our period so that by 1850 (if not before) couples were really choosing on a personal basis either how much sex to have (fully realising the consequences) or even how many children to have. Flandrin's belief that much of the French fertility decline stemmed from changed ideas about the status of women and children [24], and various impressionistic hints that certain groups adopted a more pleasure-seeking attitude to sex [61; 65], are both compatible with this position. Fertility, however, would remain high even under these circumstances unless the costs and benefits of small families improved. Only for a few groups in our period does this seem to have become the case.

(iv) CHANGES IN MARRIAGE PATTERNS

The final factor to be discussed is marriage, both the ages at which women married and the proportions who did so. Recent work has strongly emphasised the significance of these variables as the most important general mechanism of constraint in largely pre-contraceptive societies, and also as key variables in changes over time.

The importance of a peculiarly Western European marriage pattern as a constraint on population growth was first noted by Hajnal [2a]. Hajnal pointed out that in the later nineteenth century Western Europe was characterised by a pattern which, when compared with Eastern Europe and with most of the non-European world, showed markedly delayed marriage (average ages at first marriage for women being in their mid-twenties) and relatively high levels of celibacy (with typically 10–20 per cent of women not marrying within their fertile period). Subsequent work has suggested that in the mid-nineteenth century well over half of women's total potential fertility was being 'lost' in most countries through celibacy and delayed marriage.

Similar patterns go back in most places to medieval times or even earlier and certainly dominate the whole of our region in our period. For example, in France, women born around 1700 had a mean age of first marriage of 25 or 26 and about 8 per cent of women did not marry before the end of their fertile period; a roughly similar pattern was present in England and Sweden. Within all these countries, however, there was considerable variability between different social groups. This pattern is clearest in the Nordic countries where, partly because of superior records, the greatest effort has been made to differentiate between the experiences of different sections of the population. A number of Scandinavian studies have shown a clear tendency for lower class men to marry somewhat older wives than did the higher social groups; in a number of places a high proportion of the poorest groups actually married women older than themselves, and there is some evidence that this practice consciously reflected a desire to hold down completed family sizes [e.g. 79; 67].

The crucial importance of marriage patterns in changing national birth rates has been most dramatically demonstrated for England. In their original work on this topic Wrigley and Schofield [7; 9] suggested that the proportions never marrying fell from about 27 per cent for cohorts born around 1650 to about 10 per cent of the group born in the 1700s and below 5 per cent of those born around 1740. A subsequent rise still left the figure below 10 per cent for all groups born before 1800, and only a little higher for the rest of our period. In parallel, reconstitutions showed the mean age of marriage for women falling from about 26.8 years for the cohort born around 1640 to a low of 23.8 for those born around 1790, then rising rapidly among those who married in the second quarter of the nineteenth century. The combined effect of these changes, Wrigley and Schofield argued, explained over 80 per cent of the rise in fertility between the late seventeenth and the early nineteenth centuries (and nearly three-fifths of all the rise in population growth).

Unfortunately, there are uncertainties in the parish register data for this period, the age at marriage data come from just thirteen reconstitutions, and the proportions never married are estimated by a method which makes some susbtantial assumptions. More recently, Weir (*Journal of Family History*, 1984) has shown by simulation techniques that Wrigley and Schofield's estimates of birth rates, ages at marriage, and proportions never marrying are not consistent with each other, particularly for groups born around 1740 and around 1790.

Schofield [56] has taken up this point, conceding that the calculated ages at marriage for the later cohorts are the most fragile. He has produced revised estimates that involve only small changes in proportions ever married. But the revised figures stress even more strongly the crucial role of variations in the age of female first marriage as a cause of eighteenth-century population growth. In the revised figures mean age at marriage falls from 25.3 for women born around 1716 to 22.6 for women born around 1791 (the falls are particularly due to rising proportions of women marrying at young ages–see [57]); there is then a sharp rise to 25.3 for the 1816 birth cohort.

An even greater liberalisation of marriage patterns, with even more dramatic consequences, has frequently been suggested for Ireland. In particular, Connell [12] suggested that the principal cause of the rapid Irish population growth of the eighteenth and early nineteenth century was a low age of marriage which in turn produced very high levels of fertility. Connell's evidence for the eighteenth century was almost entirely of an anecdotal kind and his views have been strongly criticised (see Drake, *Economic History Review*, 1963) on the grounds that they are contradicted by the marriage age evidence which can be deduced from the 1841 census. Connell himself, however, was not unaware of this objection, and more recent scholarship has tended to support his belief that the decades immediately preceding the 1845 famine had seen a slowing of population growth associated with a rising age of marriage (for a discussion see [13]). If this was indeed so, then a mean age of marriage in the very early twenties in the later eighteenth century, but rising during the following decades, would still remain the most plausible cause of the extremely rapid population expansion in Ireland in the first half of our period.

In the case of England and Ireland, then, changing marriage patterns have been seen as a major element accelerating population growth in the eighteenth century and slowing it in the nineteenth. Elsewhere, however, changes in marriage behaviour over the first two-thirds of our period seem on balance to have acted as a brake on population growth. Extensive data for France show a mean age at first marriage for women rising by around one year over the second half of the eighteenth century, then falling back in the early decades of the nineteenth. In parallel, the proportion of women dying unmarried after the age of 50 rose from about 8 per cent of those born around 1700 to about 13 per cent of women born a century later; there then followed a small fall as fertility limitation within marriage became increasingly the prime French method of population control [76; 77]. By contrast, in Sweden, a slow rise in celibacy in the eighteenth century accelerated over the early decades of the nineteenth so that some 19 per cent of women born around 1850 remained unmarried, this being a significant factor reducing Swedish population growth over the later years of the century. The age of marriage seems also on average to have risen, though not by enough to be of much demographic significance. A similar pattern of rising celibacy seems to have occurred in Norway and (at least outside Flanders) in Belgium.

(v) CONCLUSIONS

Fertility was a key variable in the differing patterns of population growth in Europe in our period. In different places, and among different groups of the population, however, the mechanisms underlying fertility change were rather different. The extent to which these differences reflect different economic and social structures and transformations will be taken up in the last two chapters of this book.

7 Mortality

Recent research has played down the significance of mortality as the key determinant of European growth rates in our period. Nevertheless, its widespread fall remains important, though explaining it still poses considerable problems. However, one frequent cause of difficulties can largely be discounted. The crude death rate is often a poor indicator of mortality experience because it fails to allow for changes in the proportions of populations which are in the highest risk age groups. Fortunately, in our period, the limited evidence on age-specific mortality rates suggests that the major trends and turning points in mortality are well reflected by crude death rate changes, though some fluctuations in the crude rate may be due to these 'compositional effects'.

(i) CRISIS MORTALITY

Much early work focused on changes in 'crisis mortality'. Flinn [3; 41] argued that crises dominated the demographic system of Early Modern Europe, with about 3 per cent of the population dying in a 'normal' year but, perhaps as often as once a decade, this level doubling or trebling; more rarely, over restricted areas, a third or more of the population might die. For Flinn, a reduction of the incidence and severity of these mortality surges was crucial to the death rate fall of our period.

As we saw earlier, before 1700 epidemic disease was a major crisis killer and even after 1720, when plague finally disappeared from our area, local epidemics of smallpox, dysentery, typhus, measles and influenza continued. Occasionally, as in England in 1741–2, these local surges in infection spread widely enough to produce a significant crisis on a national scale. However, the greatest national mortality disasters of the Early Modern period were associated not with disease but with warfare and famine, both of which often brought epidemics in their train. The Great Northern War of 1700–21, with the disease and disruption to food supplies that followed, probably killed 20 per cent of the population of Sweden [18]. In the famines of the 1690s at least a fifth of the population of Finland, and perhaps 10 per cent of Scots, died [18; 11]. France lost around two million people in the crisis of 1693–4, and another million in 1709–10 [23].

This, however, was the last nation-wide subsistence crisis in France, though there were at least six regional crises before 1815, and food shortages occurred quite frequently right up to 1853. Some reduction in the severity of national mortality crises also occurred elsewhere, especially after the 1770s. Indeed, by the early nineteenth century, even major military operations or harvest failures often passed without serious consequences. Thus, the European-wide harvest shortages of 1816 doubled or trebled grain prices but there were major surges in mortality only in Switzerland and Southern Germany, and then only of around 60 per cent above normal [45]. Prompt administrative action prevented catastrophe after the serious harvest shortages in Scotland and Sweden in 1782–3 [11; 43]; it also saved Scotland and Belgium from disaster after the potato failure of the 1840s. Except in parts of Scandinavia (where there were also problems in the 1770s and 1780s), improved army administration and tactics meant that even the vast military operations of 1792–1815 did not hit the civilian populations in the manner of the wars of a century earlier [41].

We can get some idea of the scale of crisis mortality if we compare the peak annual crude death rate in any decade with the median figure for that decade. In England between 1700 and 1750, the peaks exceeded the medians by between 17 per cent and 42 per cent; the average of the five decades was 27 per cent. For 1750–99, by contrast, no decade had a peak more than 18 per cent above its median, and the average excess was only 10 per cent; for 1800–49 the maximum excess was just 12 per cent and the average only 7 per cent (computed from [71]). Even brief crises were declining in England in this period. In only fourteen separate *months* between 1750 and 1799 did mortality move more than 25 per cent above a 25-year moving average trend. In the next half century it did so on just four occasions.

Nevertheless, local mortality surges continued even in England. Precise over-time comparisons are difficult because increasing parish sizes reduced the chances of mortality surges arising from purely random fluctuations. However, on Wrigley and Schofield's figures, crises at parish level fell by nearly one-third between 1675–1725 and 1800–24, from around ten 'crisis months' per 1000 months observed to around six [7].

Elsewhere, while the situation improved, it did not in general do so as markedly as in England. France experienced a clear fall in fluctuations, but between 1800 and 1849 the peak death rates for the five decades still averaged 13 per cent above the decadal medians [from 43a]. Experience elsewhere was even less favourable. Scotland, in the trade depression years of 1837 and 1847, suffered serious epidemics of typhus and other hunger- and crowd-related diseases; these probably raised national mortality by over 50 per cent and doubled urban death rates [11]. Denmark, where decadal peaks averaged 20 per cent above decade medians for 1750–99, had peaks averaging 23 per cent above medians for 1800–49; only the 1840s had a peak of less than 10 per cent (computed from [15; 91]). The Swedish death rate doubled in the epidemics and hunger following the harvest failures of 1771 and 1772, and Sweden's experience after 1800 was boosted by the 85 per cent peak mortality of 1809; in no decade was the excess below 10 per cent [from 17]. In Iceland, volcanic eruptions spread ash on the pasturelands, and around a fifth of the population died in 1783–4 alone [16]. The Finnish death rate reached 60 per 1000 for 1809–10 and the failure of the potato in the late 1840s caused a further surge [43b]. In Ireland, in the same period, the potato crisis probably killed, directly or indirectly, over a million people [47].

When viewed across the continent as a whole, therefore, the significance of a decline in crisis mortality has perhaps been exaggerated. Certainly, by the end of our period, national or regional crises of subsistence were confined to years of major economic dislocation and, in the main, to poorer and geographically or politically peripheral areas. This, however, was largely already the case by the 1780s and had been so to a great extent even earlier. Moreover, with a few exceptions to be discussed below, local epidemics seem to have fallen only gradually. In England, 13 per cent of Wrigley and Schofield's 404 parishes had significant mortality surges between July 1783 and June 1784, and over 10 per cent in each year between July 1831 and June 1833. But even these contemporaneous local crises, in the aggregate, pushed *national* mortality rates only a few percentage points above the trend. There was, however, nothing new about this. In fact, both in England,

and to a great extent elsewhere, long-run death rates had often moved against the trend in major mortality crises [7]. In our period, as in earlier times, it was thus mainly changes in non-crisis, 'background mortality' which brought the death rate down.

(ii) BACKGROUND MORTALITY

The evidence on background mortality is much more fragmentary, and we have to use comparative analysis between countries, and between areas within countries, to provide the only real clues for our interpretations.

One set of clues is provided by *changes in the age structure of mortality*. The most reliable long-run data come from Sweden where infant mortality(measured as the number of deaths in any year per thousand children born in that year) hovered around 200 for the 1750s, fell slowly until the early nineteenth century, then declined more rapidly after about 1810, reaching around 150 by the 1850s. Mortality in the 1–4 age group fluctuated in the eighteenth century, peaked in the 1770s, then fell sharply, checked around 1800, and descended rapidly after 1810; by the 1840s its level was only around 60 per cent of the 1750–99 average. Similar falls occurred in Sweden among older children and adolescents. Among adults, and particularly adult men, however, any clear decline was delayed until the 1840s, and the early-nineteenth-century mortality of older age groups was actually above the mid-eighteenth-century level [17; 43c]. In Finland, infant mortality fell steadily over our period, from about 225 per 1000 births in 1750–75 to around 190 by 1826–50. Deaths at other ages, by contrast, showed if anything a tendency to rise [20].

French age-specific mortality data exist on a decadal basis throughout our period, but interpretation is clouded by ignorance over the age distribution of unregistered deaths. Clearly, though, French infant mortality was very high until the 1780s or 1790s, with rates of around 280 per thousand births. Thereafter a rapid decline began, to around 180 by the 1820s and 155 by the 1840s [22; 43a]. In contrast to Sweden, however, all age groups up to about 50 shared in a substantial decline; young adults were already experiencing improved survival chances by the 1780s; for children, however, as for infants, there was little amelioration before the last years of the century.

Elsewhere, information is less complete but similar trends are apparent. Infant and child mortality fell in Geneva between 1770–90 and 1800–25, the greatest improvements occurring among 1–4 year olds and in the 10–19 age group [e.g. 43a]. In thirteen English parishes, the infant mortality rate for children born between 1700 and 1749 lay in the range 169–195 (depending on assumptions about the effects of delayed baptism). For 1750–99 it was 133–165. By 1846–50, in spite of massive urbanisation in the intervening period, the *national* rate (including cities) was around 150 (after allowance for under-registration of births). Clearly, much of the English mortality decline over our period came from reduced infant mortality [9].

What happened to English *child* mortality is more uncertain. Some fall is apparent between the first and second half of the eighteenth century in the thirteen parishes studied by Wrigley and Schofield [9] (though this was mainly confined to the 5–9 age group). However, the national mid-nineteenth-century figures were significantly higher than Wrigley and Schofield's late-eighteenth-century estimates, presumably due to the rural bias in their parish collection.

It seems likely that infant mortality fell in Scotland, though the basis for this is slender [11]. Danish and Finnish infant mortality probably fell markedly between the 1780s and the 1830s [4b; 52], and the same seems true of South Flanders [4d].

In sum, reductions in infant and perhaps child deaths were an important component in national mortality declines. Even in France, where adult mortality clearly improved, more than 80 per cent of the improvement in life expectancy between 1760–9 and 1820–9 resulted from falling mortality among children under 10; the figure for Sweden is similar [43a]. Whether infant and child mortality improvement was so important elsewhere is uncertain. In most parts of Germany, and in some local studies of other urban and industrialising areas, an opposite trend has been observed [63; 43d; 43e; Knodel and de Vos, *Journal of Family History*, 1980]; in Germany this has been attributed to increased and more continuous employment of women in field labour [43e] and elsewhere especially to increasing population densities [e.g. 63]. Mokyr's suggested figure for Ireland of 223 per thousand births for 1836–40 might also suggest a rise in the years before the Famine, but the figure seems implausibly high when compared with other areas of Europe at this date and may well be an overestimate [47].

A second set of clues comes from some unexpected patterns in *social differentials in mortality*. Peasant mortality in some parts of Sweden was not very different from that of the poor, and several local studies suggest that nineteenth-century infant mortality among farmers' children actually exceeded that of the rest of the population, while proletarian infant mortality fell faster than that of the peasantry [43c; 50; 52; 66]. At a very different social level, the European aristocracy, like much of the rest of the population, experienced improved survival prospects over the eighteenth century; for example, between 1700–49 and 1775–99 infant mortality among the children of the English peerage fell by half with a further fall of a fifth by 1825–49 [44]. Smaller falls also occurred in child mortality, though among adults improvement was slower, particularly for males.

A third set of clues, from *causes of death*, involves very uncertain ground since we frequently lack reliable information, partly because cause was seldom systematically recorded, and partly because medical diagnosis focused on symptoms since underlying causes were not understood. Even famine deaths pose problems, for few people were ever reported as dying of starvation, presumably at least in part because hunger increased case mortality from many diseases such as measles, tuberculosis and some intestinal infections [39a; 43b; 43f].

In the case of some diseases, however, the picture is now fairly clear. In particular, it now seems incontrovertible that smallpox mortality fell markedly over our period, though whether from a reduced incidence of the disease or from decreased case fatality remains debatable. Before its decline, smallpox was a major killer. In Sweden, measles and smallpox together contributed at least 13 per cent of all deaths in the late 1750s, and smallpox alone at least 11 per cent in the late 1770s [43c]; by 1795–9, however, only around 6 per cent of all deaths were from smallpox, and after 1815 only 1 per cent. In Scotland, smallpox deaths probably fell somewhat in the eighteenth century, but in Glasgow it still caused 19 per cent of deaths of children under 10 in the 1790s [11]. By 1801–6, however, the Glasgow figure was only 9 per cent of all child deaths and for 1807–12 a mere 4 per cent (though, as in some other areas, there was some resurgence in the 1830s and 1840s). Smallpox deaths also fell sharply in parts of Norway and

Denmark after 1800, though the disease was by no means eradicated, and the fact that Finland could produce a major epidemic in 1803 suggests strongly that the disease itself was not lessening in virulence (Turpeinen, *Annales de Demographie Historique*, 1980; [43]).

Smallpox is particularly relevant to our analysis since it killed mainly children. One review of the Swedish figures for 1779–82 [50] suggests that 28 per cent of all smallpox deaths occurred to children under one year of age, 51 per cent to children aged 1–4 and another 15 per cent to children of 5–9; in Glasgow half of all smallpox deaths involved children between six months and two years [11]. However, some scholars have argued that declining smallpox mortality was demographically unimportant, since very young children, saved from smallpox, would have died instead from other diseases (particularly measles and, later, scarlatina) [43e; 3]. In Germany, where infant mortality remained high, this could have been true, and Glasgow certainly had bad measles epidemics after smallpox declined. In Sweden, by contrast, measles and whooping cough deaths also fell in the second half of our period, further reducing child mortality [50].

On most other major killers, evidence is contradictory or almost totally lacking. Typhus may have declined somewhat but epidemics could still recur in bad years. There is no sign of any fall in water- and food-borne intestinal diseases such as dysentery and typhoid; indeed they may have increased. Finally, mortality from lung tuberculosis probably rose for much of this period, though deaths were falling in England by the 1840s; the fact that tuberculosis, which caused 11 per cent of all deaths in Sweden in 1779–82, remained so high is especially interesting because its main victims were adults, and especially older men and young women, groups whose overall mortality fell only very slowly if at all over our period [42; 50; 3; 11].

The analysis so far thus provides the following clues: there was a widespread geographical distribution to the decline in mortality; it occurred in almost all social groups; the fall was particularly vigorous among the very young while among adults the mortality reduction tended to be delayed; smallpox, an infant killer, declined, while lung tuberculosis, a killer of adults, probably increased in many areas; extreme mortality crises lessened (particularly in England and France) but smaller and more localised mortality surges remained. These, then, are the essential background facts to

surges remained. These, then, are the essential background facts to any valid assessment of explanations of the mortality changes of our period.

(iii)   EXPLANATIONS OF MORTALITY DECLINE

For most older writers, it was simple. Our period saw substantial advances in medical education, in hospital and dispensary provision, in numbers of medical personnel, and the first major exercise in preventive medicine: inoculation and then vaccination against smallpox. Town improvement and better personal hygiene were also important [summary in 10].

In the 1950s and 1960s, however, McKeown demolished most of this medical interpretation [42]. With a few minor exceptions, he argued that, until well after 1850, doctors could do little to reduce mortality; this was particularly so if (as was true in the nineteenth century) the key element in the mortality decline was a fall in death from air-borne infections. Even in 1850 doctors had no real understanding of infection; before the twentieth century effective treatments were available only for a few numerically unimportant conditions; nineteenth-century hospitals were hotbeds of infection and probably increased mortality. Modern medical experience even cast doubts on the effectiveness of vaccination in the control of smallpox, unless accompanied by rigorous surveillance and isolation of contacts; until the last years of our period there was, says McKeown, insufficient coverage of the population against smallpox to be effective, and a false belief that vaccination gave lifetime immunity. Inoculation (involving the use of attenuated strains of the smallpox virus) could well have spread infection as much as it prevented it.

In assessing McKeown's writings we should note that they are based on three assumptions which have been proved questionable by recent research. Firstly, he believed that he had to find death rate explanations for most of the eighteenth-century population rise in Europe; he thus dismissed some arguments simply because they could not account for enough of the changes which occurred. Secondly, he was unable to take account of the age and cause-of-death information now available, particularly for Sweden. Thirdly, much of McKeown's interpretation relied on backwards extrapolation from often rather poor later nineteenth-century statistics, and he assumed that the eighteenth century saw the start of a single two-century process of European-wide demographic change; many would challenge that idea today [7; 4e; 43c; 59].

The role of medicine in the mortality decline must certainly have been limited and folk practices continued to have wide support among the mass of most populations. Nevertheless, eighteenth-century hospitals provided nursing care which might well have kept some of the cold and hungry alive, while the more efficient setting of fractures would have helped to get many wage-earners back to work and thus improved the nutritional levels of their families [53].

There was also increased concern by doctors and public authorities with private and public cleanliness, particularly from the late eighteenth century; however, there was little effective, legislatively supported, action, and there was also widespread evasion, at least before 1850 [43g; 49]. Increased overcrowding in older areas probably offset most of the planning benefits of new urban areas and, though agrarian reforms dispersed some Nordic populations from dense insanitary villages, relatively few people were involved. Cheaper cotton clothing and more soap may have improved personal cleanliness, but though this may have reduced typhus mortality, 'as a defence against diseases such as typhoid and cholera ... the washing of hands is about as effective as the wringing of hands' [42b, *540*].

Smallpox raises more controversy. McKeown's views have been vigorously challenged by Razzell, who originally attributed most of the English population growth to *inoculation* using the attenuated smallpox virus [49]. Subsequently, and controversially, Razzell has played down *vaccination*, using cowpox virus, arguing that inoculation continued in use; interestingly, this might have provided life-long protection and have thus made 'vaccination' more effective than in the modern world.

There is certainly persuasive evidence of the local effectiveness of inoculation, and the introduction of widespread vaccination in Europe after 1800 closely paralleled a major fall in smallpox mortality (see Mercer, *Population Studies*, 1985). However, deaths were probably falling in Sweden before inoculation began in the 1780s, having risen in the previous half century [43c]. Deaths also dropped in eighteenth-century Norway and Denmark, even though preventive measures were not widely attempted before 1800. Anyway, the spread of vaccination in Norway was too slow to explain the mortality reduction (less than half of all children were covered before 1830) [21]; in Scania in southern Sweden effective coverage probably followed rather than preceded the mortality decline [43c].

Was better childcare or better nutrition reducing mortality? Nutritional status is not normally considered important in smallpox resistance, but, for diseases like measles, tuberculosis and cholera, modern medicine stresses its significance [39c]. McKeown [49] argued for the paramount importance of improved nutrition in the later nineteenth-century mortality decline and, by extension, for our period also. Flinn supports this view [3], pointing to extended areas of cultivation, new crops, better transportation and marketing and more sophisticated administration of food supplies. For Flinn the main improvements come from reduced starvation, but for McKeown the crucial causes were improved initial resistance to infection, a greater ability to fight the disease, and lowered susceptibility to subsequent infections.

McKeown's views have recently been questioned even for the nineteenth century, and he is vague about the levels of malnutrition involved. For our period, though there are places where nutritional improvement did occur, there are others where it almost certainly did not; moreover, generally, throughout the period, the correlation between price and mortality fluctuations is weak. It is also implausible that improvements in nutrition occurred widely enough to explain the parallelisms of timing in the fall in mortality, since the mortality decline occurred roughly simultaneously across countries and regions with very different paths of economic development [4a, 43a]. In Denmark agrarian reform and technical changes produced considerable per capita increases in food supply between 1770 and 1800 and this may have helped people to fight disease [4b]. In most areas of Sweden, however, in spite of agricultural innovations, real wages probably fell in the later eighteenth century, and in Scania the fall in mortality was slower in those places where real wages were higher [43c]. In parts of Germany where food availability increased fastest, the death rates remained high [4c]. English real wages show no clear sign of improvement between 1755 and 1810 and only modest advance before the 1820s, while agricultural output fell behind population growth for most of the period [95].

In some areas, larger average family sizes might also have offset much of the earlier standard of living improvements. Increased heights of adolescent children of London labourers, however, have been interpreted as indicating improved nutrition before 1790 and after 1810 [39b], but Scottish diet shows little improvement between the 1790s and the 1840s [6]. Possibly nutrition might have improved because the available food was more evenly spread across the population, possibly changing social attitudes meant that children benefited from a more equal distribution of food within families; but all this takes us into the realms of high speculation.

There are also other objections to a nutrition-based explanation. Tuberculosis mortality probably increased over most of our period yet tuberculosis is generally believed (especially by McKeown) to be highly nutrition-sensitive; a nutrition argument would not lead us to expect a mortality decline widely spread across all social groups; reduced exposure to infections, suggested by McKeown for the aristocracy, seems far fetched [42; 49; 43a; 43c]. However, even aristocratic children may have been underfed for customary reasons in the eighteenth century, a point meriting further research.

One version of the nutrition thesis requires special consideration: the possible life-saving effects of the potato, cultivation of which spread across most of our area in our period. Potatoes provided a cheap source of food readily grown even on inferior land; they had a high calorific content and, cooked in their skins, were a significant source of protein, of certain minerals and of vitamin C (discussion in [4f]). By 1835 at least one-third of all the energy intake of the Norwegian population came from potatoes, and in Ireland and parts of Scotland and Finland they were even more important.

Did they also provide an important insurance against grain harvest failure, being more reliable because they could tolerate a wider range of growing conditions than grains, and perhaps even (as was apparently the case with maize in southern France) doing better in years when the more traditional staple crops were poor, and *vice versa* [3; 11]? This hypothesis is not well researched since it needs high-quality agricultural output data. Norwegian research, though using poor data, supports the hypothesis (discussed in [4f]), but Mokyr's investigations of French harvest data suggest that the potato was a *less* reliable crop overall and that it tended to do badly in bad grain harvest years [in 48]. Anyway, grain and potatoes were normally grown by different groups for different purposes, and logistical and financial difficulties limited simple substitution in bad years [47].

Moreover, there are doubts as to whether potato cultivation for

8 Population and Resources

The previous four sections have examined the various elements that contributed to population change over our period. To understand these changes fully, however, requires an exploration of the interaction between the components, and an investigation of their relationship to long-term economic change.

The model generally employed by students of animal species other than man sees short-run population movements and long-term population sizes as 'density-dependent'. As population rises, the incidence of disease and predation increases more than proportionally, while *per capita* access to resources like food and breeding sites falls. Some zoologists have argued that preventive mechanisms exist by which animal populations limit their numbers to the resources available, but this view is now discredited. Instead it is argued that animals have an inherent tendency to multiply until they meet an ecologically bounded ceiling at which high levels of disease and predation, and exhaustion of food, reduce population to a level well below the peak. The cycle then begins again.

Malthus, though not the first, is certainly the most cited scholar to have applied such principles to human populations. In his *Essay on the Principle of Population* he wrote as follows: '1. Population is necessarily limited by the means of subsistence. 2. Population invariably increases where the means of subsistence increase, unless prevented by some very powerful and obvious checks.' [35; *18*] Malthus recognised that human populations could modify their ecological environment by cultivating their own food but he believed that man's ability to increase food production would always be lower than his own capacity to increase. Man's special characteristic, rationality, might allow population growth to be limited by encouraging celibacy or delayed marriage among those who could not provide for their offspring, but Malthus was pessimistic that this 'preventive check' would ultimately be powerful enough to restrain population growth.

However, famine was not the only alternative check on population growth. There were other 'preventive checks' through what he calls 'vice' (he hints at prostitution, birth control and abortion or infanticide), and there were other 'positive checks' including 'excesses of all kinds, the whole train of common diseases and epidemics, wars, plague, and famine'. Indeed, Malthus seems to have seen larger populations as operating under greater pressure, and consequently as more likely to succumb to a range of vices and misery.

The ambiguities yet richness of Malthus's analysis have led authors to use 'Malthusian' principles to inform many different and sometimes inconsistent styles of analysis. One approach is to seek to identify situations where populations outrun the means of subsistence and to look for correlations between high mortality and high-price/low-income years. There is, however, a general difficulty in employing Malthusian notions of positive check in this way since, for the most vulnerable sections of the population, the crucial determinants of starvation are often not the means of subsistence available to the society as a whole, but the pattern of income distribution and the effectiveness of the social welfare and crisis support systems [39a; 40].

We should not, therefore, necessarily expect to find close connections between economic conditions and high mortality since many other factors can intervene. For our period, indeed, Malthusian interpretations of mortality fluctuations have in general been unfashionable; for example, Wrigley and Schofield [7] argue persuasively that the positive check was almost totally absent in England after 1700. In Sweden, however, recent research has suggested a link between real wage fluctuations and mortality fluctuations even after 1800, though these correlations seem at a local level to be strongest in the *same* year. This suggests that the crucial element may have been the weather, independently reducing the harvest and increasing mortality through disease [43h; 43i]. Moreover, since Swedish population was rising in this period, oscillations were taking place against a rising trend; any simple notion of population limited by 'the carrying capacity of the land' is thus inappropriate since, although population rose, crises did not get worse. The same phenomenon is apparent in France, and Richards (*Demography*, 1983) has argued that temporarily high wheat prices merely hastened deaths of already weak children rather than raising the trend level of mortality.

How about major crises such as the Swiss mortality of 1816–18 and the Irish famine of the 1840s? Superficially these were clear retributions for overpopulation, but several authors cast doubts on this (though they adopt rather different approaches to the Malthusian analysis). Many have stressed the need in the analysis of famines to avoid judgements which employ knowledge available only with hindsight [e.g. 37]. For example, in retrospect, Iceland might have suffered less in 1783–4 had her population been smaller, but a volcanic eruption on the scale which occurred could not reasonably have been foreseen; overpopulation cannot therefore be blamed for the disaster. A similar analysis for Ireland argues that blight was an unforeseeable phenomenon and that the famine was thus exogenously induced [37]. In the Irish case, however, others have replied that only an overpopulated society would have been so dependent on a single crop and have noted that there had been sixteen partial potato failures between 1800 and 1844; there is, however, debate over whether these can legitimately be treated as warnings [see 13].

Doubt on the overpopulation of Ireland has also been cast by direct international comparisons of the availability of resources per head, and of their links to population growth. Ireland was not, in European terms, particularly densely populated and, after the Famine, lower population did not markedly increase living standards. In addition, on Mokyr's figures at least, there is no clear direct connection between density and/or poverty in any region and higher than average levels of infant mortality [47].

A Malthusian retort might be that a less populated Ireland would have been wealthier, have had better food reserves, and have been able to move more food to the starving. Clearly, the development of improved transportation and marketing did reduce famine in Europe in the eighteenth century, with the result that higher population densities could be supported [3]. Lack of surplus for storage (plus the fact that potatoes could not be stored) was obviously important in Finland, while transport distance was crucial for Iceland, and post-war disorganised markets played a part in the central European crisis of 1816–17 [43b; 16; 45]. However, as Boserup has pointed out, transport improvements and market development may in part be 'stimulated' by high population density [38]; also, high-density populations, being more difficult to control if they rioted, were more likely to engender organised assistance by

67

elites. The connection between population density and famine relief is thus ambiguous.

Ireland, however, had food. In the early 1840s a quarter of her total agricultural output was exported, enough to feed more than a million people [48]. Exports continued even in the famine years, but they were mainly grain from the capitalist farms of the east. To a great extent, then, the problem in Ireland, Finland and the Scottish Highlands, was not so much of inadequate food in normal times as of more general economic underdevelopment, poor administrative and marketing infrastructure, and unequal distribution of resources. Ireland, argues Mokyr, starved because she was poor, but the poverty stemmed from lack of investment and low labour productivity rather than overpopulation [47].

Malthus's arguments may also apply to non-crisis situations. The model is a dynamic, self-equilibrating one, in which rising population reduces living standards and subsequent readjustment may come either through preventive checks or, more drastically, through increased mortality. Since, in either case, the link is through reduced access to resource-generating niches in society (or, more directly, through reduced income within them), much attention has focused on possible changes over time in the direct connections between population levels and resources.

The establishment of reliable measures of overpopulation and its consequences is difficult. A valuable synthesis is provided by Grigg [37]; he investigated a number of 'symptoms of overpopulation' including increased landlessness, subdivided farms, rising rents and falling wages, and ploughing of marginal land. Grigg's conclusion for our period is that population increase imposed considerable stress on the means of subsistence in most of Western Europe; by the 1820s and 1830s there was widespread evidence of overpopulation. Grain prices rose and real wages were widely depressed, often only recovering to their 1750s levels around the end of our period; in many areas (and particularly in parts of France, Ireland and much of Germany) subdivision of farming units was rampant; landlessness became a major concern in much of Scandinavia; in Belgium and parts of Germany, and probably widely elsewhere on the continent, urban workers experienced a deterioration in the quality and range, and arguably also the quantity, of their diets. Yet major crisis was largely avoided. Even the Irish Famine should, in Grigg's view, be attributed to a great extent to the incompetence and indifference of the British government's attempts to organise relief. So, if overpopulation was widespread, how did Europe escape?

One safety valve for overpopulation is temporary or permanent emigration, but, as we have seen, it was not widely used until after the end of our period (except, perhaps significantly, in Ireland). The situation of the peasantry in some areas, and particularly in France, was helped by a reduction in the incidence of taxation as a result of the reduction of feudal privileges during the period of Revolutionary rule; the extent and effects of these changes are, however, poorly researched and it is difficult to assess their full significance. A third ameliorating factor was the movement of underemployed masses to the towns, where mortality was much higher, but this, certainly by the end of our period, played only a small role in reducing population pressure.

Instead, four other routes saved most of the continent from calamity. Firstly, as Malthus himself recognised, in 1750 most of the people of our area were living at significantly above a 'subsistence' level. In England, the population stagnation of the previous hundred years had been accompanied by slow but significant economic growth and by rising agricultural productivity; as a result, living standards had risen somewhat and could be squeezed in the later eighteenth century without disaster striking most of the population. A similar cushion was widely available elsewhere as a result of the demographic crises of the first half of the century, and through the still widely available possibilities of taking new lands into intensive cultivation by land reclamation and improved drainage or by carving out new plots from the forests. As a result, the full rigour of demographic pressures generally struck only after the Napoleonic wars, and even then were mitigated by further expansions of the cultivated area.

Secondly, in many areas a significant expansion of previously very low levels of non-agricultural employment provided incomes for those for whom there was no room on the land; because much of the new employment focused on exportable commodities, it allowed substantial imports of basic foodstuffs and thus provided a growing section of the population with the means of subsistence by routes which Malthus largely ignored. By 1850, as a result, economic growth was faster almost everywhere than population growth itself, and average living standards were rising. The areas which experienced the greatest population pressures during our period

69

mostly lacked major industrial expansion. Ireland, indeed, suffered some de-industrialisation as cotton and linen came under competition from mainland Britain [47].

This would not have mattered if Irish agricultural output had expanded rapidly enough to feed the growing population. Boserup has argued [38] that population pressure is the greatest stimulus to agricultural change and particularly to the development of higher productivity, more intensive agriculture. This was clearly a third factor at work in our period, as rising demand across the continent encouraged both peasants and landowners to alter methods of land holding and utilisation and, particularly, to reduce the extent of fallow through the introduction of new crops and the break-up of communal systems of farming; the widespread adoption of the potato was a popular response of a similar kind.

Agricultural innovation, however, normally requires profitable markets and thus a strong cash demand for food and this was by no means everywhere apparent; certainly progress was often desperately slow, particularly in areas dominated by large numbers of small peasant landholders. In many places, had the potato not become available, it is not clear that alternative, more investment-intensive forms of enhanced food production would have developed. More likely, population growth would have slowed, either through catastrophic mortality of the kind that occurred in the late seventeenth century, or through increased operation of the preventive check. It is indeed an interesting observation on Boserup's analysis that some scholars have suggested that population pressures in France in this period, associated as they were with high density and very small landholdings, may actually have discouraged the consolidation and enclosure of open fields because of fears about the lack of viability of the ensuing plots.

The preventive check was the fourth escape route in our period, and a vital one since it kept population growth in most areas well below that of the currently developing world and thus allowed economic growth to take most of the strain of growing numbers. A cultural (and at times a legal [4c, 21]) requirement that one should have a niche in society before entering into 'licensed' procreation meant, as we have seen in an earlier section, that late marriage and widespread celibacy were a traditional Western European device by which population and resources were maintained in some rough kind of balance [7]. Was this preventive check also variable in response to population pressure?

Certainly, in Sweden, there are suggestions that the rising celibacy of the eighteenth century was a response to population pressure, and it also seems possible that fertility limitation through nuptiality and contraception was being employed in some densely populated parts of the Netherlands by the 1840s. Some scholars have argued that the emergence of fertility limitation in France in the eighteenth century represented a different kind of phenomenon from the widespread fertility reductions of a century later, and that it had Malthusian origins. Dupaquier [23] has pointed to the rising age at marriage in France in the eighteenth century, and its parallels with falling real wages and extending subdivision; nuptiality changes were, he suggests, a traditional reaction to population pressure. However, as Wrigley has recently argued [59], even in the later eighteenth century they were inadequate to keep population growth within reasonable bounds and they were dramatically overthrown by the encouragement to marriage produced by the exemption of married men from military service during the Napoleonic wars. Under these circumstances, deliberate fertility limitation became the only alternative, though a further (debatable) factor may have been a desire among the peasantry to reduce family size to avoid the worst consequences of Napoleonic partible inheritance laws [78].

However, the chronological connection between resources and the preventive check has been explored most explicitly for England, where fertility limitation within marriage was not well developed in our period. Wrigley and Schofield [7], plotting long-term population growth against a real wage index, observe a lagged pattern in which population growth responded only slowly to changes in real wages. The key determinant of changes in population growth was the marriage rate, which lagged, they suggest, thirty to fifty years behind real wage cycles. Wrigley and Schofield explain their observation by suggesting that, because short-run fluctuations in economic conditions were considerable, long-term changes in conditions only became apparent after a considerable lapse of time; conventions about acceptable marriage circumstances thus changed relatively slowly. Thus, for example, improvements in living standards in the 150 years after 1620 were still raising marriage rates in the late eighteenth century and still producing a birth rate surge up to 1816, even though the real wage had by then been falling for at least half a century. Reactions to this fall were similarly delayed, so that only in the late eighteenth century did a stronger preventive check begin to operate on marriage, and only later still did population growth rates begin to fall.

This interpretation has been widely criticised [see e.g. 54; 55; 57]. The lags seem to some critics implausibly long and not as apparent in the evidence as the authors imply. The real wage index is an imperfect one and does not correspond well with more recent calculations. An 'average' real wage index can anyway only poorly reflect the changes in circumstances favourable to marriage which may be experienced among substantial sectors of the population. This is particularly the case in a period such as ours when substantial shifts of population were occurring into the waged sector, when dependence on new forms of wage income was increasing, and when marked changes were taking place in income distributions and standard of living expectations [57].

In a recent article, indeed, Schofield has emphasised rather different factors from those stressed in *The Population History of England* [56]. He suggests that in our period it was through changes in the *age at marriage* (rather than in the proportions marrying) that the preventive check mainly operated, and he suggests that changing expectations of long-term living standards may have been a crucial variable. Expanding opportunities in the eighteenth century encouraged a marriage age fall, but in the nineteenth century the age of marriage rose as expected standards of living increased with a shift in the occupational structure away from agricultural labour and into craft and service occupations. Even more important were the increased constraints on family support introduced by the New Poor Law of 1834 with their depressing effect on the perceptions of those contemplating marriage after that date.

Wrigley and Schofield's work also reminds us of the inverse side of Malthus's analysis: rising population would increase misery, but exogenous increases in living standards would encourage earlier and more universal marriage and thus accelerate population growth. In many interpretations, this was the European-wide impact of the potato, since it opened up opportunities by reducing the minimum size of viable holdings; this subdivision encouraged earlier marriage which allowed population growth [3; 12; 21; 64; 65]. For Ireland, this position remains subject to debate, since long-term trends in marriage ages and the timing of the spread of the potato are obscure [46; 13]. Economic change could also expand marriage opportunities through other mechanisms. Schofield's recent paper brings him nearer some earlier writers who suggested (both for England and elsewhere) that marriage changes in our period have frequently reflected changed employment opportunities and especially the increasing availability of rural domestic handicraft (or 'proto-industrial') employment [e.g. 56; 61; 63; 64; 65].

The general argument was characterised neatly by Medick when he wrote [61] that domestic industry, organised on a putting-out basis with the putter-out providing all the materials and equipment, allowed 'the possibility of forming a family primarily as a unit of labour'. In contrast to a peasant or artisan economy where skill and capital had to be obtained before a niche could be acquired, proto-industrial families, engaged in relatively unskilled tasks, had few external constraints over the timing of their marriages; they also had incentives to marry (and to marry young) so as to establish a balanced productive unit and exploit peak earning capacities. Contemporary comment was widespread in Europe about the prevalence of 'beggar weddings' between 'people who have two spinning wheels but no bed', as one Swiss commentator wrote [cited 65].

Quantitative support for these impressions is weak but in Flanders the ages of men and women at first marriage fell faster in the areas where domestic linen production was introduced in the eighteenth century than in areas where it did not appear [64; 2c]; marital fertility was also higher in the linen-producing areas. Similarly, in the framework knitting village of Shepshed in Leicestershire, proto-industrialisation was followed by a fall of over three years in the median age of marriage for women [63].

In both Flanders and Shepshed, however, the good times did not last. In Shepshed a glutted market for labour and increasing trade cycle insecurity produced major adjustment problems, and Levine claims (though, as we have seen, the evidence is not wholly convincing) that active fertility limitation was employed well before 1850 [63]. In Flanders where, according to Mendels, it was population pressure which encouraged the development of linen manufacture in the first place, the resultant demographic regime rapidly expanded population and symptoms of overpopulation reappeared [64]. And, more widely, and especially after 1800, disruptions of trade through war or the sudden imposition of tariffs, shifts of fashion, and competition from factory production frequently led to a collapse of incomes among densely populated and now largely landless proto-industrial workers; the result was widespread distress.

It was not only proto-industry, however, which offered opportunities of freer entry into marriage. Availability of new land through forest clearance allowed low marriage ages in Finland, agrarian reforms opened up new marriage opportunities in Denmark, and land reclamation did the same in the Netherlands. Any form of wage labour which does not require celibate cohabitation with the employer may free individuals to marry if adequate resources to house and support a family can be obtained. As Goldstone [57] has recently pointed out, a plausible explanation of the rapid rise in the proportion of women in England who married at very young ages is that development in both the industrial and the agricultural sectors of the eighteenth-century economy provided many new employment opportunities for proletarian workers. Similarly, several authors [esp. 60] have suggested that the eighteenth-century shift in England towards agricultural day labour directly produced younger marriage and lower rates of celibacy, but this assumes that constraints like housing shortages and decreasing opportunities for married women's agricultural employment did not have opposite effects. Schofield [56] suggests instead that new Poor Relief policies, focused on supporting families with children, may have been of key importance in eighteenth-century England; direct attempts to link such policies with population growth rates have not, however, proved very successful (e.g. Huzel, *Economic History Review*, 1980).

Certainly, we should not assume that proto-industrialisation and proletarianisation will automatically lower marriage ages, particularly for women (and see [62] and Jeannin, *Annales, Économies, Sociétés, Civilisations*, 1980). Changes in labour demand do seem to have lowered marriage ages in some English villages [63], but Swedish research shows that the landless tended to have older wives than did peasants; indeed, as we saw in an earlier chapter, their wives were frequently older than themselves [66; 67]. This was also noted in Norway by Sundt who was told that this was deliberate, with the object of reducing fertility to a level compatible with the appallingly low earnings of landless men [21; 79]. Freedom from property constraints, therefore, did not *necessarily* lead to younger marriage. Resources, and especially expectations about

74

future living standards were crucial. The preventive check was thus a powerful and variable controller of Europe's population growth in our period.

9 Economic and Social Implications

The previous section concluded that the mechanisms of economic change and demographic control worked well enough in most places to prevent population growth from reducing the living standards of the mass of the population to a subsistence level. Some countries, however, and England in particular, did substantially better than this: there was real economic growth. England, in a period of rapid demographic change, also experienced the onset of the world's first 'industrial revolution', a shift to sustained, industry-led economic growth, associated with major changes in the scale and organisation of production. By 1850 similar transformations were also getting under way over much of the rest of Western Europe. Could the demographic growth have been a *causal* factor in these economic changes?

A number of scholars have answered in the positive, the extreme expression being Hicks's remark that 'perhaps the whole Industrial Revolution of the last two hundred years has been nothing else but a vast secular boom, largely induced by the unparalleled rise of population' [cited in 94a]. Others, more cautiously, have seen population growth as a significant contributor to economic change in England [6; 10; 60; 94c]. By contrast, few continental scholars lay much emphasis on positive economic consequences of population growth in our period (see also the judicious comments in [96, *chap. 2*]); some French writers, however (especially Chaunu writing about Normandy, *Annales, Économies, Sociétés, Civilisations, 1972*) have stressed the deleterious effects on economic development of an absence of demographic pressures. Our discussion thus follows the literature in relating particularly to the British Isles; even here, however, a more sceptical view has recently emerged [e.g. 94b].

England, of course, was, in the traditional view, exceptional. Taking the early 1750s as our starting point, a variety of recent writings may be summarised as suggesting that total measurable output (GDP) rose by about 60 per cent to 1810, by well over 150 per cent by 1830 and by well over 350 per cent by 1850. Output per head was at least a tenth higher by 1800, a quarter higher by

1830 and over 50 per cent higher by 1850.

Modern estimates such as these, it should be noted, suggest much faster growth in the nineteenth than the eighteenth century, and only a limited impact of new forms of production as late as 1850. This alone cautions against attributing too much to mid-eighteenth-century changes in population growth. Moreover, while new modes of production developed more slowly elsewhere, recent work on France, in particular, has suggested rates of economic growth not very different from those of Great Britain. The fact that the French economy could expand so rapidly in spite of France's slow population growth suggests that connections between demographic and economic changes in this period are far from simple [and see 96].

Doubts have also been expressed on theoretical grounds. Older explanations particularly stressed the impact of population on demand. However, while population growth increases the total volume of *desired* goods and services within an economy, if these desires are to be translated into economic growth the 'supply side' of the economy must develop to provide resources which the extra population can employ to generate *effective* demand [e.g. 94b]. This requires supply side adjustments which are not necessarily forthcoming (the extra people may just join the starving unemployed). More significantly, for the extra demand to generate economic growth *per capita*, the adjustments must overcome the tendency for the marginal productivity of labour to fall; otherwise, the extra labour lowers the average productivity (and thus the average remuneration) of the economy. It is therefore essential that investment increases at a rate faster than population growth, and that substantial technical advance occurs; there is no theoretical reason why population pressure should induce these. Indeed, in the alternative view, it was only because they were taking place anyway that population growth could continue.

An alternative demand side view has seen the initial demand stimulus of population change as operating more indirectly via entrepreneurial expectations. An economy where mortality fluctuations were reduced and where population was growing was likely to be seen as offering profitable opportunities for investment; resources which would otherwise have gone unemployed would thus be invested in capital goods of a productive kind, and this investment would stimulate further economic expansion [93]. However, while, in retrospect, it is clear that investment in Britain in the later eighteenth century was less risky than it had been earlier, this may well not have been apparent much before 1840. Such an analysis thus seems more applicable in Britain after 1840 when living standards per worker were more clearly rising. Interestingly, many modern interpretations also stress this as the crucial period of economic change [e.g. 95].

A series of supply side explanations has also been proposed. Rapid population growth leads, all other things being equal, to a fall in wages; labour inputs thus become cheaper. This encourages entrepreneurs to develop new ventures (though economic theory predicts that these would involve relatively labour-intensive forms of production); the widespread expansion of domestic industry might indeed by explained in these terms, but ready supplies of cheap labour should have acted as a deterrent to the adoption of capital-intensive but labour-saving developments associated with mechanised production; yet these developments, perhaps quite erroneously, play a major role in most interpretations of eighteenth-century economic change in England; regional labour shortages in areas like Lancashire may nevertheless have been enough to stimulate developments of this kind. However, for similar reasons to those developed above, extra labour will only generate growth *per capita* if it is either accompanied by an increase in the investment ratio or, in the short run, if it allows otherwise underexploited resources to be fully employed; the role of population is at best secondary.

There are, of course, subtler ways in which population growth may operate. Rising population reduces rigidities in labour markets by encouraging mobility of underemployed resources and by ensuring that there is a supply of new labour available for training for new jobs as they arise; as a result labour for expanding opportunities does not have to be dragged away from less productive employments. In England, rising fertility and improving child survival meant that almost one extra child per family grew to adulthood in the period 1800–25 compared to the years 1725–50 [98]. In England and many parts of Germany, and quite widely elsewhere (except, significantly, in France), new labour or productive units were bound to be arising and this clearly opened up possibilities for the introduction of new forms of production; again, however, such possibilities did not *have* to be taken up and, indeed, in many parts of our area such as Scandinavia they were largely ignored until after the end of our period.

A growing population also has a larger proportion of its members in the younger age groups and this is often seen as encouraging dynamism as well as providing a fitter and stronger labour force [93]. This is, however, offset by higher numbers of children, but they are less demanding consumers and, for most of our period, could play some productive role from a relatively young age. Interestingly, in England, the proportions of adults aged 15–59 in the population probably declined until the 1820s so that economic growth up to that point took place against a worsening dependency ratio [7]; thereafter, however, the period of more rapid growth coincided with improved dependency ratios but also with the onset of cyclical bouts of unemployment. The precise role of changing age structure is thus unclear.

Finally, two other effects of expanding populations have been suggested. Higher aggregate demand from larger populations may encourage improved productivity through economies of scale; concentrations of population may reduce 'transaction costs' per head [93]. As far as production is concerned, however, it seems that the technical, financial and organisational constraints of our period operated at such small levels that national population changes were not relevant [94b]. On the other hand, greater population densities (and particularly more concentrated markets) might have made feasible transport extensions and information developments (such as local newspapers) which would not otherwise have occurred. These developments would significantly reduce transaction costs across a range of goods and services and could well have been important, though the main source of improvement was urbanisation rather than population growth. Similarly, while the costs of most forms of public administration and of the provision of social capital such as water and sewerage and public buildings did not rise linearly with population, the great administrative and public works revolutions came to most of Western Europe, including Britain, only after the end of our period.

Even more complex arguments have been put forward, suggesting possible effects on demand for industrial products of relative shifts in agricultural and industrial incomes and costs, and of relative incomes of employees and employers [see e.g. 94c]. These arguments, however, are dependent on unknown factors such as a possible socially differential impact on consumption patterns of rises and falls in income. Falling incomes may, however, be offset by greater effort or greater involvement of women and children in the

79

market economy. Evidence is almost totally lacking on most of these points.

At present, then, there is little reason to believe that population growth in our period played a substantial independent role in accelerating economic change. Once such changes were occurring, population change may have made a useful supporting contribution, especially once living standards began to rise significantly. Most important, however, was the fact that in most areas population growth kept below the rate of investment and of technical change; it thus did not positively inhibit growth. Ireland may be an exception, but some scholars at least have argued that Ireland's problems came more from lack of investment than from population growth. Elsewhere, in Scandinavia for example, continued high natural increase after 1850 did not prevent economic growth from occurring at rates much faster than in our period. We should not, therefore, use high population growth as a major factor holding back countries such as Sweden from economic development earlier in the century (useful summary in [4a]).

How about possible wider *social* implications of demographic change? Clearly, the expansion of national populations and the rapid growth which occurred at some local levels posed a range of administrative, economic and social problems; it also helped to dissolve older forms of production and social life (the arguments are reviewed for Britain in [98]) and arguably even played an indirect role in the onset of the French Revolution (good discussion in [96]). Many rural areas could not have stood the strain of higher population densities without compensating changes (for example, the supplementation of family incomes by rural industry, the expansion of forms of employment particularly absorptive of young persons – notably domestic service – the introduction of new foodstuffs which allowed the subdivision of plots, or the arrival of agrarian reforms which brought higher productivity from new forms of land tenure or labour exploitation). Frequently, these changes were associated with others such as a change in family labour strategies (which might involve either more or less female field labour depending on the area), and the breakdown of older village-based control over many aspects of social life [e.g. 43c; 43e; 64; 65; 96].

Population pressure (or at least the fear of it) also induced significant reforms in social welfare; these sometimes, as in eighteenth-century England, may have encouraged marriage by favouring married male employment and supporting family incomes; sometimes (as in England after 1834) they might seek actively to discourage family formation. In a number of areas more direct attempts were made to limit marriage (though this often increased cohabitation and illegitimate births) [4c, 19].

Occasionally, and particularly in Ireland in the 1840s and Germany in the 1820s, demographic events had a more dramatic effect, splitting families and communities permanently through widespread overseas emigration on a scale much larger than in previous periods; whether this permanently changed the social structure of these societies is, however, open to dispute. Even in less troubled times, one response to rising population which seems to have expanded significantly in our period was seasonal migration.

Changing birth and death rates also had more independent effects. Urban death rates generally remained substantially above those of country areas (and this acted as a major stimulus to attempts at sanitary reform), but they fell enough to allow considerable urban growth to take place through natural increase; this was vital in the rapid urban expansion after 1800 when in many areas the share of the countryside in total population was contracting and rural population surplus alone could not have produced the growth that did occur [5]. Another important side-effect, equally important in many countries in rural areas as well, was that most of the rapid expansion of the wage-earning proletariat could take place through its own natural increase. Europe's growing proletariat thus grew up in proletarian households and culture, rather than being torn away from peasant or craft production, with unpredictable results [97].

The most spectacular changes, however, occurred at the level of personal survival, though the consequences are more difficult to infer. 'Expectation of life at birth' (the average number of years lived) probably increased in England over our period from around 36 to around 41 years. In Sweden the increases were from 38 to 46 years, and in Denmark, between the 1780s and the 1840s, from about 35 to 44 years. The most dramatic changes occurred in France where the rise was from 29 to 41 years. At the level of personal and family experience, however, it is more relevant to note the effect of this on *survival*, particularly among infants and children. In England about 23 per cent of boys born in the early 1740s died before their first birthday and half were dead by about age 28. By contrast, only about 16 per cent of boys born in the early 1830s died in infancy and half only by age 44 [98]. In France, where infant mortality fell from 29 per cent to 17 per cent of those born, survival of the 1830s cohort was roughly the same as in England; but this was a dramatic contrast compared with the half of those born in the 1750s who died by the age of nine [22]. These changes have led some scholars to ask whether improvements in child survival may have changed parents' perceptions of their children.

More generally, however, because adult survival changed little in our period compared with the dramatic improvement of the next hundred years, the impact through changes in social experiences, in orphanhood, in abilities to make realistic plans ahead, was probably less than it later became [98]. Nevertheless, the general reduction in major demographic crises clearly did change expectations somewhat. This is nowhere better revealed than in public reaction to those mortality surges which did occur, such as cholera in 1831–2 and 1848–9, or the threats of mass starvation in Scotland in the late 1840s [51; 11; 3]. People were no longer *expected* to die in massive numbers from sudden and unpredictable causes. This fact alone, perhaps, demonstrates the significance of the population changes of north-western Europe in the century before 1850.

Select Bibliography

This list of works is intended to provide a basic introduction to the literature (particularly the literature in English) on topics covered by this book; it is not an exhaustive list of the works used in preparing the text.

The place of publication is London unless otherwise stated.

(A) GENERAL COLLECTIONS AND SURVEYS

[1] E. A. Wrigley, *Population and History* (1969). Still the best general introduction to the historical demographer's task.
[2] D. V. Glass and D. E. C. Eversley, *Population in History* (1965). A major collection of essays of continuing significance. Note especially chapters by Hajnal [2a], Utterström [2b], and Deprez [2c].
[3] M. W. Flinn, *The European Demographic System 1500–1800* (Brighton, 1981). A masterly synthesis which, however, underplays the variations demonstrated by more recent work.
[4] W. R. Lee (ed.), *European Demography and Economic Growth* (1979). A useful collection. Note especially the introduction [4a], and the chapters by Andersen [4b], Lee [4c], Deprez [4d], Fridlizius [4e], and Drake [4f].
[5] J. de Vries, *European Urbanization, 1500–1800* (1984).

(B) NATIONAL SURVEYS

[6] N. L. Tranter, *Population and Society, 1750–1940* (1985). A useful if uneven survey, best on sources, on migration and on economic and social implications.
[7] E. A. Wrigley and R. S. Schofield, *The Population History of England, 1541–1871: a Reconstruction* (1981). Though this pioneering masterpiece is written with great clarity, the density and range of material covered can be daunting on first reading. The overall argument can be fairly well grasped by focusing

initially on the introduction, followed by chapters 6, 7 (up to page 269), 10 and 11. Useful reviews are in *Social History* (1983), *Population Studies* (1983), *Journal of Economic History* (1983) and *Population* (1983). See also [54] and [55].

[8] E. A. Wrigley, 'The growth of population in eighteenth-century England: a conundrum resolved', *Past and Present*, xcviii (1983). A summary, for our period, of the core of the argument of [7].

[9] E. A. Wrigley and R. S. Schofield, 'English population history from family reconstitution: summary results 1600–1799', *Population Studies*, xxxvii (1983). An essential companion to [7].

[10] M. W. Flinn, *British Population Growth 1700–1850* (1970). Mostly now superseded by [7], but still excellent on source problems and useful on economic implications.

[11] M. W. Flinn *et al.*, *Scottish Population History from the Seventeenth Century to the 1930s* (1977). Shows, comprehensively, how much is yet to be learnt.

[12] K. H. Connell, *The Population of Ireland, 1750–1845* (Oxford, 1950). Still the fundamental work on Ireland from which all others start.

[13] J. Mokyr and C. Ó Gráda, 'New developments in Irish population history, 1700–1850', *Economic History Review*, xxxvii (1984). A useful survey of research since [12].

[14] J. M. Goldstrom and L. A. Clarkson (eds), *Irish Population, Economy and Society* (Oxford, 1981). The chapters by Clarkson [14a] and Lee [14b] are especially useful on source problems.

[15] H. Gille, 'Demographic history of the North European countries in the eighteenth century', *Population Studies*, iii (1949).

[16] R. F. Tomasson, 'A millenium of misery: the demography of the Icelanders', *Population Studies*, xxxi (1977).

[17] *Historical Statistics of Sweden*, Part 1: *Population 1720–1950* (Stockholm, 1955).

[18] G. Utterström, 'Some population problems in pre-industrial Sweden', *Scandinavian Economic History Review*, ii (1954).

[19] A. Lassen, 'The population of Denmark, 1660–1960', *Scandinavian Economic History Review*, xiv (1966).

[20] O. Turpeinen, 'Fertility and mortality in Finland since 1750', *Population Studies*, xxxiii (1979).

[21] M. Drake, *Population and Society in Norway 1735–1865* (1969).

[22] 'Démographie Historique', *Population* special number to xxx (1975). Contains a series of important summaries of the French aggregative project.

[23] J. Dupaquier, *La Population française aux XVII et XVIII siècles* (Paris, 1979). An excellent short survey.

[24] J-L. Flandrin, *Families in Former Times* (1979). Mainly on French family life, but with interesting if controversial ideas on fertility and mortality reduction.

[25] W. R. Lee, *Population Growth, Economic Development and Social Change in Bavaria, 1750–1850* (New York, 1977).

[26] K. B. Mayer, *The Population of Switzerland* (New York, 1952).

(c) Sources and techniques

See also [7, 11, 14, 21, 23]

[27] T. H. Hollingsworth, *Historical Demography* (1969). Rather fragmented, but invaluable on sources.

[28] P. G. Spagnoli, 'Population history from parish monographs: the problem of local demographic variations', *Journal of Interdisciplinary History*, vii (1977).

[29] E. A. Wrigley (ed.), *An Introduction to English Historical Demography* (1966). On methods for aggregative analysis and family reconstitution with English records. See especially chapters 3 and 4.

[30] A-S. Kälvemark, 'The country that kept track of its population: methodological aspects of Swedish population records', *Scandinavian Journal of History*, ii (1977).

[31] K. Pitkanen, 'The reliability of the registration of births and deaths in Finland in the eighteenth and nineteenth centuries', *Scandinavian Economic History Review*, xxv (1977).

[32] P. Thestrip, 'Methodological problems of a family reconstitution study in a Danish rural parish', *Scandinavian Economic History Review*, xx (1972).

[33] M. P. Guttman and P. Wyrick, 'Adapting methods to needs; studying fertility and nuptiality in 17th and 18th century Belgium', *Historical Methods*, xiv (1981). Short cuts for partial family reconstitution.

[34] J. Knodel and E. Shorter, 'The reliability of family reconstituition data in German villages', *Annales de Démographie Historique* (1976). On *Ortssippenbücher*.

(D) THE GENERAL DETERMINANTS OF POPULATION SIZE

[35] T. R. Malthus, *An Essay on the Principle of Population*, 2nd edn (1803) [references are to the Dent 1958 edition]. Remains essential reading for all serious students of historical demography.

[36] W. Petersen, *Malthus* (1979). Useful background to [35].

[37] D. Grigg, *Population Growth and Agrarian Change* (1980). Very useful on the conceptual issues; some flaws in the historical accounts.

[38] E. Boserup, *Population and Technology* (Oxford, 1981). Inspiring if controversial. In part an alternative view to [35].

(E) MORTALITY

See also [7, 11, 12, 13, 15, 16, 23]

[39] R. R. Rotberg, and T. K. Rabb (eds), *Hunger and History* (1983). A very useful collection of papers. Note especially chapters by Watkins and van de Walle [39a], by Fogel *et al.* [39b], and by 'the Conferees' [39c].

[40] A. K. Sen, *Poverty and Famines* (Oxford, 1981). Important conceptual and theoretical insights.

[41] M. W. Flinn, 'The stabilisation of mortality in pre-industrial Western Europe', *Journal of European Economic History*, III (1974). An excellent early survey of the issues.

[42] T. McKeown, *The Modern Rise of Population* (1976). See also review by Schofield in *Population Studies*, 1977 [42a], and McKeown's replies to critics in *Population Studies*, 1978 [42b]. This controversial book summarises work published by McKeown and his colleagues in *Population Studies* in 1955 and 1962.

[43] T. Bengtsson *et al.*, *Pre-industrial Population Change* (Stockholm, 1984). An extremely useful recent collection, particularly on Sweden. Note especially chapters by Perrenoud [43a], Kaukiainen [43b], Fridlizius [43c], Imhof [43d], Lee [43e], Fridlizius and Ohlsson [43f], Goubert [43g], Bengtsson and Ohlson [43h], and Bengtsson [43i].

[44] T. H. Hollingsworth, 'The demography of the British peerage', *Population Studies*, Supplement to vol. XVIII (1956).

[45] J. D. Post, *The Last Great Subsistence Crisis in the Western World* (1977).

[46] L. M. Cullen, 'Irish History Without the Potato', *Past and Present*, xl (1968).

[47] J. Mokyr, *Why Ireland Starved* (1983). Important, imaginative, but controversial in parts.

[48] P. Solar, 'Agricultural productivity and economic development in Ireland and Scotland in the early nineteenth century', in T. M. Devine and D. Dickson, *Ireland and Scotland 1600–1850* (1983).

[49] P. E. Razzell, 'Population change in eighteenth-century England: a reinterpretation', *Economic History Review*, xviii (1965). Stresses smallpox inoculation and vaccination.

[50] L. Widén, 'Mortality and causes of death in Sweden during the eighteenth century', *Statistisk Tidskrift*, xii (1975).

[51] R. J. Morris, *Cholera 1832* (1976).

[52] O. Turpeinen, 'Infant mortality in Finland, 1749–1865', *Scandinavian Economic History Review*, xvii (1979).

[53] S. Cherry, 'The hospitals and population growth', *Population Studies*, xxiv, i & ii (1980). A counter to [42].

(F) NATIONAL AND LOCAL POPULATION DYNAMICS

See also [3, 4, 7, 8, 11, 12, 21, 23, 47]

[54] *Journal of Inter-disciplinary History*, xv (1985) contains a symposium on English population history organised around [7]. Among many useful papers note especially those by Schofield, Lee and Lindert.

[55] P. H. Lindert, 'English living standards, population growth and Wrigley–Schofield', *Explorations in Economic History*, xx (1983).

[56] R. S. Schofield, 'English marriage patterns revisited', *Journal of Family History*, x (1985). Some revised data and a rather different interpretation from [7].

[57] J. A. Goldstone, 'The demographic revolution in England: a re-examination', *Population Studies*, xl (1986).

[58] M. K. Matossian, 'Mold poisoning and population growth in England and France, 1750–1850', *Journal of Economic History*, xliv (1984). Provocative though probably wrong.

[59] E. A. Wrigley, 'The fall of marital fertility in nineteenth-century France: exemplar or exception?', *European Journal of Demography*, i (i & ii) (1985).

[60] H. J. Habakkuk, *Population Growth and Economic Development since 1750* (Leicester, 1971). Still worth reading for insights.

[61] H. Medick, 'The proto-industrial family economy' *Social History*, iii (1976). Conceptually important.

[62] R. Houston and K. D. M. Snell, 'Proto-industrialization? Cottage industry, social change, and industrial revolution', *Historical Journal*, xxvii (1984). A useful corrective to some of the wilder ideas on this topic.

[63] D. Levine, *Family Formation in an Age of Nascent Capitalism* (1977). A pioneering study of English villages.

[64] F. F. Mendels, *Industrialisation and Population Pressure in Eighteenth Century Flanders* (New York, 1981).

[65] R. Braun, 'Early industrialization and demographic change in the Canton of Zurich' in C. Tilly (ed.), *Historical Studies of Changing Fertility* (Princeton, 1978). Fascinating but impressionistic data.

[66] I. Eriksson and J. Rogers, *Rural labour and population change* (Uppsala, 1978). An imaginative Swedish study.

[67] C. Winberg, 'Population growth and proletarianization' in S. Åkerman *et al.*, *Chance and Change: Social and Economic Studies in Historical Demography in the Baltic Area* (Odense, 1978).

[68] R. M. Netting, *Balancing on an Alp: Ecological Change and Continuity in a Swiss Mountain Community* (1981).

(G) FERTILITY AND NUPTIALITY

See also [7, 9, 12, 23, 59, and 61–68]

[69] R. A. Bulatao and R. D. Lee (eds), *Determinants of Fertility in Developing Countries* (1983). A collection of papers with the latest data and ideas on the general determinants of fertility. See especially vol 1, chapters 1–7.

[70] C. Wilson, 'Natural fertility in pre-industrial England 1600–1799', *Population Studies*, xxxviii (1984).

[71] L. Henry, *Anciennes Familles Genevoises* (Paris, 1956). The pioneering family reconstitution study, and the first to show significant fertility limitation in pre-industrial populations.

[72] L. Henry, 'Fécondité des mariages dans le quart sud-ouest de la France de 1720 à 1829'. *Annales Economie, Société, Civilisation*, xxvii (1972). The first regional report from the important

French family reconstitution project. For the rest of the country see [73–75].

[73] L. Henry and J. Houdaille, 'Fécondité des mariages dans le quart nord-ouest de la France de 1670 à 1829'. *Population*, xxviii (1973).

[74] J. Houdaille, 'La fécondité des mariages de 1670 à 1829 dans le quart nord-est de la France', *Annales de Démographie Historique* (1976).

[75] L. Henry, 'Fécondité des mariages dans le quart sud-est de la France de 1670 à 1829', *Population*, xxxiii (1978).

[76] L. Henry and J. Houdaille, 'Célibat et age au mariage aux XVIIIe et XIXe siècles en France, I: célibat définitif', *Population*, xxxiii (1978).

[77] L. Henry and J. Houdaille, 'Célibat et age au mariage aux XVIIe et XIXe siècles en France, II: age au premier mariage', *Population*, xxxiv (1979).

[78] A.I. Hermalin and E. van de Walle, 'The civil code and nuptiality: empirical investigation of a hypothesis', in R.D. Lee (ed.), *Population Patterns in the Past* (1977). On France.

[79] E. Sundt. *On Marriage in Norway* (1855) [translation by M. Drake, Cambridge, 1980]. A pioneering piece of sociological investigation.

[80] D. Gaunt, 'Family planning and the pre-industrial society: some Swedish evidence', in K. Ågren *et al*, *Aristocrats, Farmers, Proletarians: Essays in Swedish Demographic History* (Uppsala, 1973).

[81] D. Gaunt, 'Pre-industrial economy and population structure', *Scandinavian Journal of History*, ii (1977).

[82] J. Knodel, 'Natural fertility in pre-industrial Germany', *Population Studies*, xxxii (1978).

[83] J. Knodel, 'Child mortality and reproductive behaviour in German village populations in the past', *Population Studies*, xxxvi (1982).

[84] J. Knodel, 'From natural fertility to family limitation: the onset of fertility transition in a sample of German villages', *Demography*, xvi (1979).

[85] J. Knodel and C. Wilson, 'The secular increase in fertility in German village populations', *Population Studies*, xxxv (1981).

[86] J. Knodel and E. van de Walle, 'Breast feeding, fertility and infant mortality: an analysis of some early German data',

Population Studies, XXI (1967).

[87] C. Wilson, 'The proximate determinants of marital fertility in England, 1600–1799', in L. Bonfield *et al.* (eds), *The World We Have Gained* (Oxford, 1986). Fascinating and important.

[88] U-B. Lithell, *Breastfeeding and Reproduction: Studies in Marital Fertility and Infant Mortality in 19th Century Finland and Sweden* (Uppsala, 1981).

[89] A. McLaren, 'Abortion in France: women and the regulation of family size, 1800–1914', *French Historical Studies*, X (1978).

[90] A. McLaren, '"Barrenness against nature": recourse to abortion in pre-industrial England', *Journal of Sex Research*, XVII (1981).

[91] T.P.R. Laslett *et al.*, *Bastardy and its Comparative History* (1980). A collection of essays with a full bibliography.

[92] E. Shorter, 'Illegitimacy, sexual revolution and social change in modern Europe' in T.K. Rabb and R.I. Rotberg (eds), *The Family in History* (New York, 1973). Controversial. Useful graphs.

(G) ECONOMIC AND SOCIAL IMPLICATIONS

see also [4, 6, 10, 24, 46, 47, 51]

[93] S. Kuznets, *Economic Growth and Structure: Selected Essays* (1966). Interesting theoretical ideas, especially in chapter 3.

[94] R. Floud and D.N. McCloskey (eds], *The Economic History of Britain since 1700* (1981), vol. 1. See especially chapters by Schofield and Lee [94a], McCloskey [94b] and Cole [94c].

[95] N.F.R. Crafts, *British Economic Growth during the Industrial Revolution* (Oxford, 1985).

[96] A. Milward and S.B. Saul, *The Economic Development of Continental Europe, 1780–1870* (1973). A wide-ranging survey with useful, often comparative discussions of social and demographic relationships with economic change.

[97] C. Tilly, 'Demographic origins of the European proletariat', in D. Levine (ed), *Proletarianization and Family History* (New York, 1984).

[98] M. Anderson, 'The social implications of demographic change', in F.M.L. Thompson (ed.), *Cambridge Social History of Britain* (forthcoming), vol.2.

Index

Note Pages marked with a star are those on which a brief explanation is given of the meaning of a technical term.

real wages   see standard of living
Rickman, J.   21
Rogers, J.   49
rural areas   25–7, 80
Russia   25

sanitary improvement   60–1, 79
Scandinavia   see Nordic countries
scarlatina   59
Schofield, R.S.   14, 18–21, 29, 33, 35, 50–1, 54–5, 57, 64, 66, 71–2
Scotland: economic change   36, 63, 68, 76–80; fertility   32, 35, 40: illegitimate   38; migration   27, 32; mortality   9, 34–5, 54–5, 57–8, 68, 82; population   22–3, 25, 35; sources and methods   11–14, 17
Shepshed   48, 73
smallpox   43, 53, 58–9, 60–2
social changes   80–2; see also attitudes
Sundt, E.   37, 74
survival   78, 81–2
Sweden: economic change   62, 64, 80; fertility   31–2, 35, 37, 40–1, 43–6, 48–9: illegitimate   38; marriage   50, 52, 71, 74; migration   28; mortality   9, 24, 31, 33–5, 37, 53-62, 64, 66: infant   45, 56, 58; population   22–5, 35, 52, 66,

80; sources and methods   11, 13, 15, 16; survival   81
Switzerland: fertility   32, 43, 48; marriage   73; migration   27; mortality   54, 57, 67; population   21–3, 25; sources and methods   11, 14

total marital fertility ratio (TMFR)   39*, 40–2, 44–6, 49
towns   14, 26, 34, 44, 55, 57, 60–1, 68–9, 79, 81
transaction costs   79
transport improvements   62, 67, 79
tuberculosis   58–9, 62–3
typhoid   59
typhus   53, 55, 59

venereal disease   43
Vic-sur-Seille   45–9

Wales: population   22–3; sources and methods   14, 15
war   9, 24–5, 27, 34–5, 37, 53–4, 66, 69, 71, 73
Webster, A.   12, 32
Weir, D.   51
wet-nursing   44
whooping cough   59
Wrigley, E.A.   14, 18–21, 29, 33, 35, 50–1, 54–5, 57, 66, 71–2